W9-BNM-028

# 2004 Yearbook

THE YEAR IN REVIEW 2003

People

# Contents




## Staff

**EDITOR** Elizabeth Sporkin **SENIOR EDITOR** Richard Burgheim **WRITERS** Michael A. Lipton, J.D. Reed, Michelle Tan **ART DIRECTOR** Brian Anstey **PHOTO EDITOR** Brian Belovitch **ASSISTANT PHOTO EDITORS** Regina Flanagan, Jen Lombardo **REPORTERS** Randy Vest (Chief), Nuy Cho, Jennifer Sobie **COPY EDITOR** Tommy Dunne **PRODUCTION ARTIST** Lisa Burnett **SPECIAL THANKS TO** Jane Bealer, Karla Borders, Ronnie Brandwein-Keats, Robert Britton, Jessica Bryan, Luciana Chang, Sal Covarrubias, Urbano DelValle, Maura Foley, Margery Frohlinger, Patricia Hustoo, Toby Kahn, Maddy Miller, Gregory Monfries, Rashida Morgan, Charles Nelson, Susan Radlauer, Annette Rusin, Jack Styczynski, Gloria Truc, Céline Wojtala, Patrick Yang

**PRESIDENT** Rob Gursha **VICE PRESIDENT, BRANDED BUSINESSES** David Arfine **VICE PRESIDENT, NEW PRODUCT DEVELOPMENT** Richard Fraiman **EXECUTIVE DIRECTOR, MARKETING SERVICES** Carol Pittard **DIRECTOR, RETAIL & SPECIAL SALES** Tom Mifsud **DIRECTOR OF FINANCE** Tricia Griffin **ASSISTANT MARKETING DIRECTOR** Niki Whelan **PREPRESS MANAGER** Emily Rabin **ASSOCIATE BOOK PRODUCTION MANAGER** Suzanne Janso **SPECIAL THANKS TO** Bozena Bannett, Alex Bliss, Bernadette Corbie, Robert Dente, Gina Di Meglio, Anne-Michelle Gallero, Peter Harper, Robert Marasco, Natalie McCrea, Jonathan Polsky, Mary Jane Rigoroso, Steven Sandonato, Grace Sullivan

82

93

63

106

40

# 2003 People of the Year

AFFLECK & LOPEZ KEPT US GUESSING, SADDAM WAS OUSTED, SCHWARZENEGGER GOT ELECTED, DEMI & ASHTON COOED, KOBE BRYANT AND MARTHA STEWART WENT TO COURT, A GAY PRIEST BECAME A BISHOP, AND THE *QUEER EYE* GUYS REIGNED AS TV'S MAKEOVER KINGS

# J.Lo & Ben

**NEITHER BAD REVIEWS NOR BAD BEHAVIOR COULD KEEP THIS PAIR—OR THE PRYING PAPARAZZI—APART**

The soap opera known as Bennifer became perhaps the most melodramatic hookup since Elizabeth Taylor and Richard Burton went flooey in the '70s. All hell broke loose in the summer, shortly after Affleck, 31, and Lopez, 34, marked their first anniversary as a couple. *The National Enquirer* reported that Ben had gotten intimate with dancers at a Vancouver strip club—the same night he and J.Lo were shown on *Dateline NBC* discussing their wedding plans. Then *Gigli,* the film on which they had met, opened to disastrous reviews ("Nearly as unwatchable as it is unpronounceable," said the *Los Angeles Times*). The lovebirds were all smiles again at Ben's 31st-birthday bash on August 16. But a few days before their scheduled September 14 Santa Barbara wedding, the couple declared it "postponed" because of all the media frenzy. Or had Ben simply gotten cold feet? Nah. Five days later, they were found nesting at his Georgia island estate. After that, the media had them on and off more often than Lopez's famous 6.1-carat, $1.1 million pink diamond engagement ring. And the Bennifer beat goes on. . . .

# Arnold Schwarzenegger

## AS WIFE MARIA STANDS BY HER MAN, THE 'GOVERNATOR' BASKS IN HIS UPSET VICTORY

"You can listen to people who have never met Arnold or who met him for five seconds 30 years ago, or you can listen to me," said Maria Shriver, adroitly deflecting newspaper reports that husband Arnold Schwarzenegger had groped numerous women. Californians obviously heeded Shriver. In October, after voting to recall the hugely unpopular Governor Gray Davis on the first question on the ballot, 49 percent chose as his successor (from 135 contenders) the Austrian-born bodybuilder turned *Terminator* star turned Republican political upstart. In his victory speech, Ah-nuld, 56, was the first to credit Shriver, 48, his fiercely loyal spouse of 17 years, mother of their four children and a Democrat-registered niece of JFK. "I know how many votes I got today because of you," he said. With his blessing, the first lady-elect declared she would shortly resume her old day job as a correspondent on NBC's *Dateline.*

# George W. Bush

**AFTER A STUNNING VICTORY IN THE WAR, THE COMMANDER IN CHIEF HUNKERED DOWN IN A LONGER, PAINFUL BATTLE FOR IRAQI PEACE**

It was a singularly triumphant image: the President of the United States standing on the flight deck of the USS *Abraham Lincoln* in May, proclaiming the end of major combat in Iraq, nearly two months after U.S. troops and their British allies toppled Saddam Hussein. The euphoria did not last. In Baghdad and other areas, peacekeeping forces were ambushed daily by Saddam loyalists and foreign terrorists. Bush, 57, came under further criticism after the failure to uncover weapons of mass destruction—a major rationale for the war. Undaunted, and unfazed by antiwar demonstrations in London, where he met with British prime minister Tony Blair in November (and inspected the guard of honor with Prince Philip, right), the President defended his policy: "In some cases," he said, "the measured use of force is all that protects us from a chaotic world ruled by force."

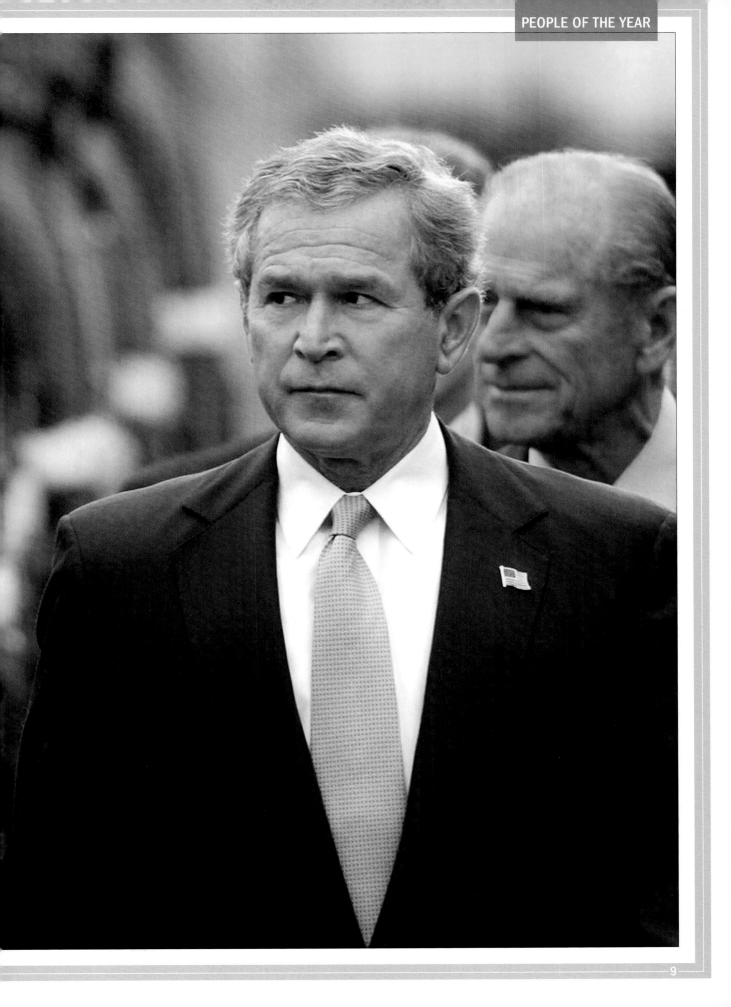

# Kobe Bryant

## HE SAID, SHE SAID: WAS IT RAPE OR WILLING SEX?

At an emotional press conference in July, Bryant, 25, the L.A. Lakers' 6′6″ superstar guard, turned to wife Vanessa (left), 21, and said, "You're the air I breathe. You're the strongest person I know, and I'm so sorry for having to put you through this." Bryant had just admitted to cheating on her with a 19-year-old Colorado hotel employee, but he vehemently denied the young woman's charge that he had sexually assaulted her in his room. "I'm innocent," he told reporters. While Bryant's role-model rep seemed permanently tarnished, it was his accuser's integrity that came under attack at a preliminary hearing in October, when Bryant's feisty attorney Pamela Mackey implied that the woman (whom she named in open court) had "had sex with three different men in three days" around the time of the alleged rape. At the Lakers' training camp the next day, Bryant denied rumors of marital discord ("You kidding me?") and said his upcoming trial wouldn't distract his game. Both at home and on the NBA court, he said, he would "take care of business."

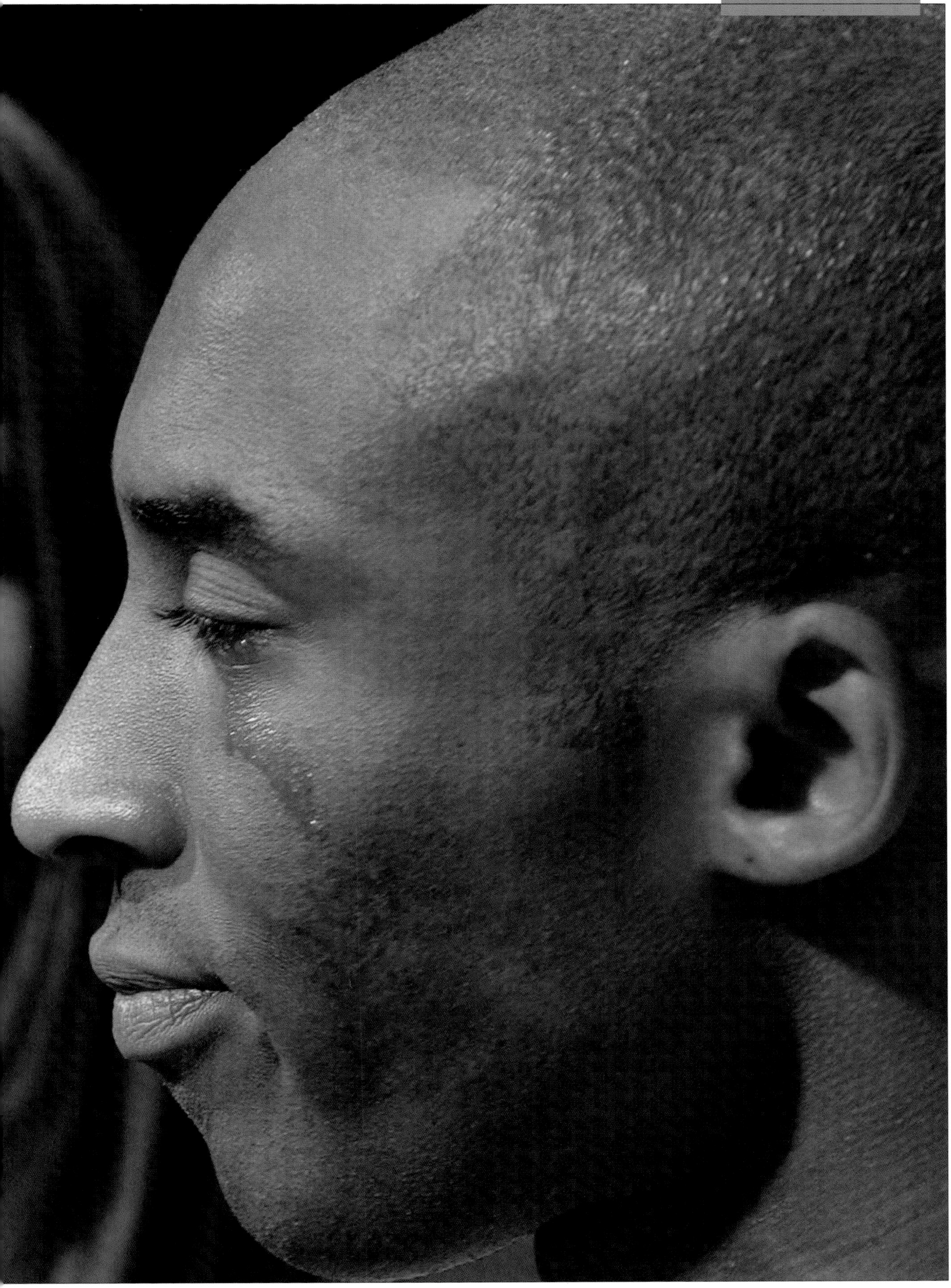

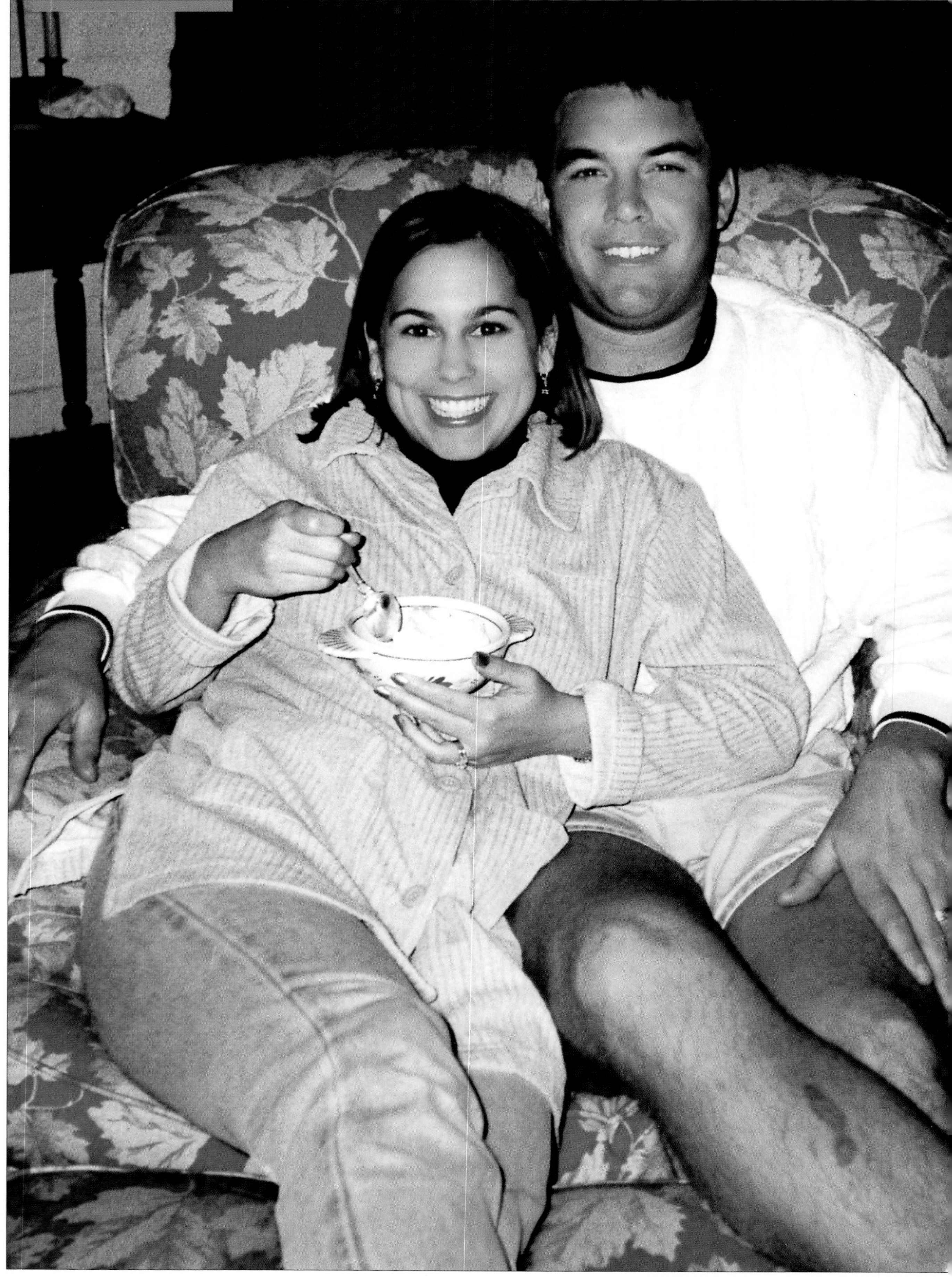

# Laci Peterson

**A PREGNANT WOMAN AND HER UNBORN CHILD WERE FOUND DEAD. WHODUNIT? HER HUSBAND WAS CHARGED, BUT HE PLED INNOCENT, AND THE CASE BECAME AMERICA'S GUILTY DIVERSION**

The year's most gripping real-life murder mystery began the day before Christmas Eve, 2002, the last time a pregnant Modesto, California, homemaker, Laci Peterson, 27, would ever be heard from. By April 14, when her mutilated corpse washed up in San Francisco Bay—a day after the body of her unborn son Conner was also discovered—Peterson's husband, Scott, 31, a fertilizer salesman, was already the leading suspect. Soon afterward, Scott was charged with Laci's murder and held without bond. The evidence against him turned out to be circumstantial: a telltale hair that might or might not have been Laci's was found in Scott's boat; the marina from where he said he'd set out to fish on December 24 was close to where the bodies were found. Prosecutors also focused on Scott's curious behavior when first questioned, such as his greater concern over the "dinged" door of her Land Rover than the fate of his pregnant wife. He had also taken out a $250,000 insurance policy on Laci (pictured with him, left, in 1997). Most intriguing was a tip from Amber Frey, 28, who had been romantically involved with Scott. On December 9, 2002, according to a detective, Peterson had told Amber that he had "lost his wife" and "this would be his first holiday without her." Frey's lawyer reported that Scott later indicated he wasn't involved in Laci's death but knew "who did it." In a surprise twist, prosecutors decided not to call Frey as a witness during Peterson's pretrial hearing. If she is asked to testify against him at his trial, "then I guarantee you that [Peterson's lawyer Mark] Geragos will go for the jugular," said one expert observer. And the public will be hooked anew.

**THE SCENE**
Laci Peterson's head and parts of her limbs were missing from her badly decomposed body when it came ashore in April.

**THE ACCUSED**
When not in court, Scott Peterson was confined to a 6-by-9-ft. cell.

**THE MISTRESS**
Amber Frey is a Fresno massage therapist and single mom.

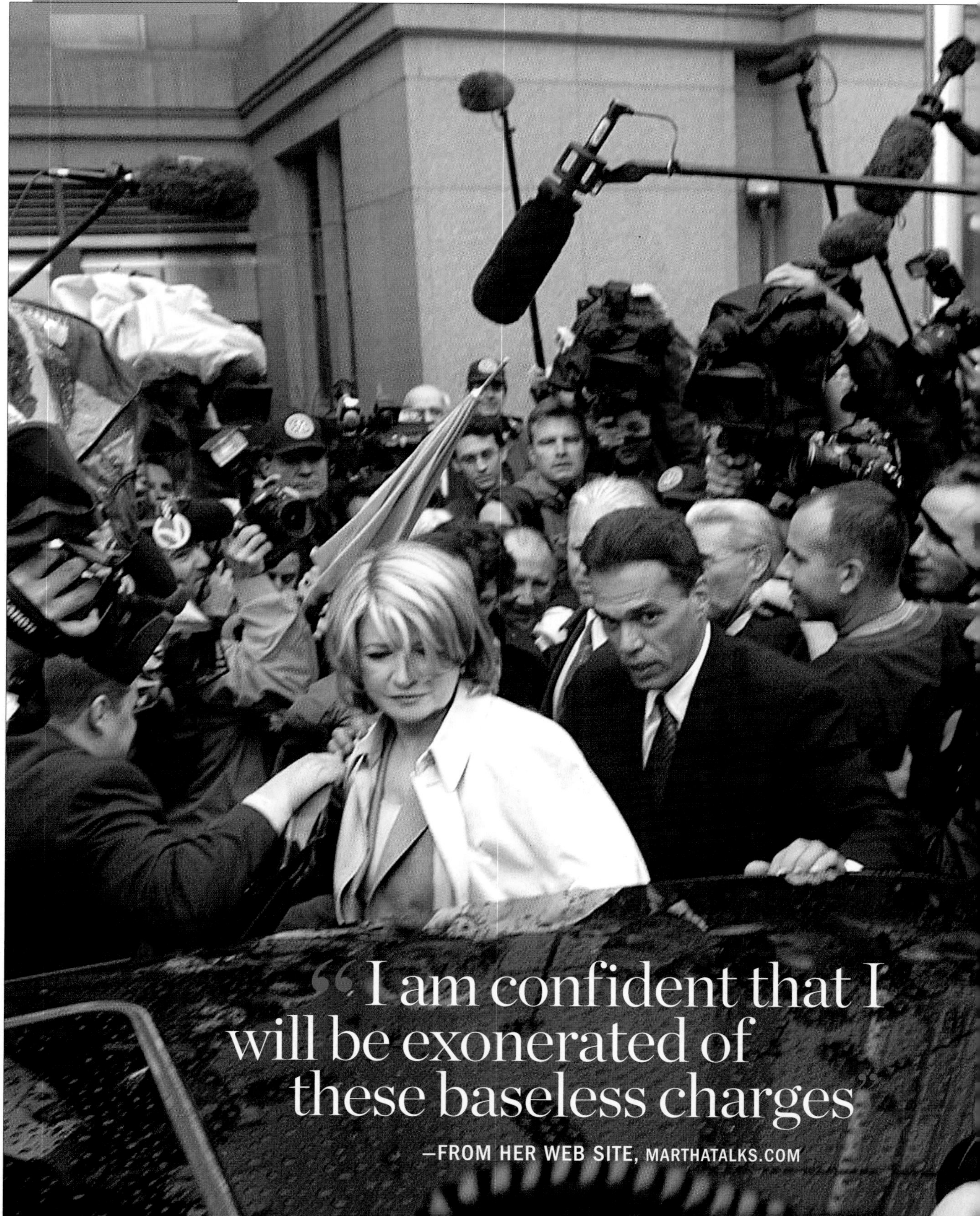

"I am confident that I will be exonerated of these baseless charges"

—FROM HER WEB SITE, MARTHATALKS.COM

# Martha Stewart

## HOLD THE STRIPES, SHE SAID; PRISON'S NOT ON HER DOCKET

No sooner had Stewart, 62, been indicted in June for obstruction of justice than the inevitable cartoons appeared, showing America's doyenne of housewares redecorating her prison cell. There was just one problem with that scenario, as Stewart saw it. "I don't think I will be going to prison," she told Barbara Walters in November. She could be right. The government's case against Stewart was based on her sudden decision to dump $228,000 worth of ImClone stock in 2002, just before it took a dive, and her alleged attempts to cover up evidence of trading on an insider tip. "This is not the strongest obstruction of justice case I have ever seen," said U.S. district judge John Sprizzo of the trial set to begin in early 2004. "This is not John Gotti." Stewart had other reasons to feel relatively positive. While her new notoriety didn't necessarily help business—circulation of *Martha Stewart Living* magazine slipped, and her syndicated TV show was banished to the wee hours in many markets—Kmart continued to push her products, and her company saw an overall 4 percent rise in profits. There were also reports of a new, *mellower* Martha. "Her old self wasn't so nice," said an East Hampton, New York, neighbor. Now, "she's more affable, smiley."

# Andrew Luster

**BUSTED IN MEXICO, HE WENT HOME TO JAIL**

His crime spree plays like a sleazy TV movie. In fact, a docudrama of his saga was being shot in Toronto in June when Max Factor-cosmetics-heir-turned-fugitive Andrew Luster, 40, was nabbed in Mexico by a U.S. bounty hunter and extradited to face justice. He had already been sentenced in absentia to 124 years in prison for the date-rape-drug assaults on three women. In addition, two of his victims were awarded $39 million in damages.

# Gene Robinson

**A GAY BISHOP CLAIMED GOD'S IN HIS CORNER—AND HIS EX-WIFE TOO**

"If at any point I felt that God were asking me not to do this, I would quit in a minute. But I have not felt that," said the Reverend Gene Robinson, 56, a few weeks before his November consecration as the Episcopal Church's first openly gay bishop. Though hailed by his New Hampshire congregation and even his ex-wife (with whom he has two adult daughters), Robinson's ascent has created a controversy in the parent Anglican Church. "We consider his election invalid," said one dissenter. Admitted Robinson: "It's going to be messy for a while."

# Elizabeth Smart

**HER NINE-MONTH ABDUCTION ENDED SAFELY**

The young girl in the flowing white robe and veil insisted her name was Augustine when police, responding to several 911 tips, stopped and questioned her in Sandy, Utah, in March, along with a robed adult couple who claimed to be her parents. "I know you think I'm that Elizabeth Smart girl who ran away, but I'm not," she said. Soon, though, she did admit she was the Elizabeth Smart who in June 2002 had been kidnapped at knifepoint from the bedroom of her Salt Lake City home by an intruder later identified as Brian David Mitchell. A onetime handyman for the Smart family and an avowed polygamist, Mitchell, 50, had allegedly targeted the 14-year-old as one of his brides. Over the next nine months, prosecutors say, Mitchell forced her to live on the streets with him and wife Wanda Barzee, 57, and sexually assaulted Elizabeth. The couple are awaiting trial. Meanwhile, Elizabeth, now 16, reunited with her parents, Lois and Ed, and her sister and four brothers and has begun her freshman year at high school. "I think there's some things different about me," she told NBC's Katie Couric, "but I think I'm still pretty much the same person."

# Judge Roy Moore

## AN ALABAMA JUDGE WENT ON TRIAL FOR BLOCKING REMOVAL OF A RELIGIOUS SCULPTURE

*Thou shalt not violate a federal court order.* Not one of the original Ten Commandments, true, but one that Moore, 56, chief justice of the Alabama supreme court, had defiantly flouted. A federal judge ordered him to remove a massive 2½-ton granite replica of the Commandments from the rotunda of the Judicial Building in Montgomery. Moore, who had had the monument installed in 2001, reacted with righteous wrath. "We're moving from separation of church and state to separation of the people from God," he told conservative supporters. In September, "Roy's Rock" was placed in storage, and two months later a judicial ethics panel voted unanimously to remove Moore as well. His parting words? "I have absolutely no regrets."

# Pete Sampras

## A GRAND OLD MAN OF GRAND SLAMS TEARFULLY HUNG UP HIS RACKET

"I'm not retiring because I'm married or [because] I have a son," Sampras, 32, told nearly 22,000 tennis fans at New York City's Arthur Ashe Stadium in August. "I'm retiring because I have nothing to prove to myself." Indeed, the genial family man (who has a 1-year-old, Christian Charles, with wife Bridget, 30) had racked up a record 14 Grand Slam singles titles since 1990—five of them at the U.S. Open, where Sampras delivered his tearful valedictory address. For six straight years he had ranked No. 1 in the world, and he went out with a victory (over Andre Agassi) at the 2002 U.S. Open. After sitting out Wimbledon in '03, he finally decided that it was "time for me to stop. I just felt like my heart wasn't into it." Now, "I'm content," he concluded at the Ashe Stadium. Among those paying tribute was fellow retiree John McEnroe. "I tried to serve like you. I couldn't do that," said McEnroe. "I also tried to act like Pete. Needless to say, I failed at that."

# Ashton & Demi

## AGE GAP BE DAMNED, THESE TWO HAD LOTS—AND LUST—IN COMMON

The cynics scoffed when Moore, 41, began stepping out with Kutcher, 25, in April. The pair, they said, were merely using the May-December age disparity to boost their careers. (In fact, despite the couple's attention-getting red-carpet arrival at the L.A. premiere of *Charlie's Angels: Full Throttle,* Demi's comeback vehicle was a box office disappointment. Nor could their red-hot romance salvage Ashton's summer bomb *My Boss's Daughter.*) The semiretired actress, with three daughters by her friendly ex, Bruce Willis, and the never-wed, A-list-aspiring *That '70s Show* hunk were said to be too incongruous to last. (No matter that Ashton doted on Demi's girls and squired Scout, 12, to the Teen Choice Awards.) Okay, then, wouldn't Willis, a regular visitor to chez Moore, get jealous? In fact, the actor, 48, had his own younger love interest, *Dog Eat Dog* host Brooke Burns, 25, and he and Kutcher seemed to get along just fine at family outings. Of one thing there was no doubt: The couple appeared as amorous in the fall as they did in May, when they ran into sexpert Dr. Ruth at the MTV Movie Awards. "From the look on their faces," the good doctor reported, "they don't need me."

# A Trio of War Heroes

"When they rescued Jessica, that gave everyone a lot of hope, because people didn't know we were still alive," recalled Shoshana Johnson (right), 30, an Army friend of Lynch's captured in the same ambush. So was Patrick Miller (center), 23, whose heroism under fire Johnson credits with saving seven POWs that day. That night, Apache helicopter pilot Ronald Young, 26, was shot down with his copilot. Marines rescued all the POWs in April. "My heart goes out to the soldiers still over there," said Young.

# Jessica Lynch

## THOUGH NO GI JANE, SHE WAS A PLUCKY SURVIVOR

The Army private's capture by Iraqi forces turned out to have been less heroic—and more harrowing—than first reported. Her convoy was ambushed, taking 11 casualties, but she didn't retaliate Rambo-style. As Lynch, 20, revealed in her memoir (a $1 million collaboration with writer Rick Bragg) *I Am a Soldier, Too: The Jessica Lynch Story,* she never fired a shot because her rifle had jammed. A Special Forces unit (tipped off by an Iraqi lawyer) rescued her from a hospital where she was being treated for multiple fractures suffered in a collision with another vehicle. Later, medical evidence indicated that she had been sexually assaulted during her nine-day ordeal. (Lynch said she had no memory of it.) By the time she finished her three-month rehab, left the Army and returned home to Palestine, West Virginia, she had become the subject of a TV movie and tabloid notoriety (*Hustler* claimed it had but wouldn't publish prewar topless photos). "I don't look at myself as a hero," Lynch told ABC's Diane Sawyer. "I'm just a survivor." With a bright future, she hoped, as a kindergarten teacher and June 2004 bride of Army sergeant Ruben Contreras, 24.

# Rosie O'Donnell

## ROSIE HELD COURT—LITERALLY—IN A NASTY LAWSUIT WHILE DOCTORING A BROADWAY 'MESS'

It was the autumn of Rosie's discontent. The former talk show diva, 41, was the major attraction in two big New York City dramas. One was her Broadway musical *Taboo,* based on the life of Boy George, in which O'Donnell, as sole producer, was a voluble backstage presence. (And why not? She had invested $10 million of her own money.) The other show was a real-life courtroom saga pitting Rosie against *Rosie,* her eponymous magazine, which folded in 2002 after she walked away. The publishers, Gruner + Jahr USA, sued her for $100 million, claiming breach of contract; she countersued for $125 million, charging that creative control had been wrested from her. Anticipating the testimony of staffers, Rosie's attorney Lorna Schofield warned in her opening statement, "She is not Mother Teresa. When she's provoked, she yells and curses." In the end, the judge ruled that neither side had proved its case. The verdict was harsher for *Taboo,* which opened one day after the end of the trial. Reviewers' reactions ranged from "lost and bereft" to "a crazy, mixed-up mess."

# Dixie Chicks

**THE GIRL BAND FOUND THEMSELVES BOYCOTTED ON THE AIRWAVES AFTER THEY DISSED THE PREZ**

It was the shot heard 'round the FM dial: "Just so you know," Dixie Chicks lead singer Natalie Maines (center), 29, told a London concert crowd, "we're ashamed the President of the United States is from Texas." That was in March, just 10 days before the U.S.-led invasion of Iraq. Suddenly the popular Dallas-based band, rounded out by banjo player Emily Robison (right), 31, and her sister, fiddler Martie Maguire, 34, got very unpopular back in the States, as radio stations temporarily banned their songs, and Maines's remark (despite her later apology) became a litmus test for the limits of dissent. Macho country star Toby Keith blasted the trio and projected a doctored image of Maines with Saddam Hussein on a large screen at several of his concerts. But the Chicks also had their defenders, including Senator John McCain (R-Ariz.), who at a hearing chastised a radio exec behind the boycott. By the summer, the controversy waned, and the Chicks waxed. They had appeared on the cover of ENTERTAINMENT WEEKLY naked except for tattoos like "Dixie Sluts" and "Proud Americans," and their album *Home* hit No. 1 on the country charts, selling a reassuring 6 million copies.

# Pamela Kaichen

## CAMERAS—AND THE FBI—NABBED A BRAZEN 'BLONDE' BANK ROBBER

She was Bonnie without Clyde. In a two-day spree in May, the raven-haired Kaichen, 43—dubbed "The Blonde Bandit" because of the wig she wore—robbed six banks in New York and Connecticut, netting more than $42,000. Caught on surveillance cameras, she was recognized five days later by a Danbury, Connecticut, cop who had previously ticketed the unemployed former horse trainer and marketing executive for failing to buckle her seat belt. He tipped off FBI agents. Pleading guilty, Kaichen faced up to seven years in prison. "She was a very good tenant," said her former landlady. "She was always giving me gifts."

# Rush Limbaugh

## THE MOUTH THAT ROARED ON RADIO WENT SILENT AS HE CHECKED INTO DRUG REHAB

His legion of Dittoheads were in mourning; his liberal detractors smirked. But Limbaugh, 52, the king of right-wing talk show hosts, played it straight—and somber. On his last radio broadcast before entering a clinic to treat his long-secret addiction to OxyContin and other prescription painkillers, Limbaugh told his 20 million listeners, "I really don't know the full scope of what I'm dealing with." The drug revelations came on the heels of another Limbaugh controversy. As the rookie commentator on ESPN's *Sunday NFL Countdown,* Limbaugh had criticized the media for overrating Philadelphia Eagles quarterback Donovan McNabb because he is black. The uproar following the remark got him booted off the network. After what Limbaugh called "five intense weeks" of rehab, he was back on his radio show, reassuring Dittoheads that he had not turned into "a linguini-spined liberal." He added, however, "I'm just like anybody else who has an addiction. I'm powerless over it and I have to continue to recognize that."

# Saddam & Sons

## IRAQ'S DESPOT WAS DRAMATICALLY HUNTED AND CAUGHT, BUT NOT BEFORE UDAY AND QUSAY WERE SHOT AND HIS DIE-HARD LOYALISTS HAD STIRRED LETHAL CHAOS IN HIS FREED NATION

In the deck of cards handed out to U.S. servicemen depicting the 55 Most Wanted Iraqis, Saddam Hussein, 66, was the ace of spades. Yet after his ouster by coalition forces, the deposed dictator remained as elusive as the Joker in *Batman*. Finally, in December, after nearly nine nerve-racking months, he was captured, harried and shaggy, near his native Tikrit. With him in his 8-ft. hole were a pistol, two AK-47s and $750,000 in $100 bills. His two sons Uday, 39, and Qusay, 37 (below, right and left), had already died in a shoot-out with U.S. troops in July, their bullet-ridden bodies put on garish display as proof of their demise. To the survivors of their sadism, it must have seemed a fitting end. Uday had tortured members of Iraq's national soccer team for subpar performances; his brother fed political prisoners headfirst into a wood chipper.

The boys had learned at home. Their father, a peasant's son who built himself some 20 palaces, had purged more than 100,000 Kurds in the 1980s, some with poison gas. And a chilling videotape from the regime's final days showed his elite Republican Guard torturing and executin[g] Iraqi troops deemed disloyal. While on the loose, Saddam released audio recordings urging Iraqis to obstruct the rebuilding of the nation. Loyalists were joined by infiltrating foreign terrorists, including possibly al-Qaeda members, leading to a greater U.S. death toll after the overthro[w] than before. When Saddam was eventually unearthed, he surrendered without a shot. Said the U.S. commanding general on the scene: "He was just caught like a rat."

# Ruben Studdard & Clay Aiken

THE *AMERICAN IDOL* WINNER AND RUNNER-UP BECAME FAST FRIENDS

Considering the photo-finish ending in May that had some fans crying foul—Studdard beat out Aiken by a mere percentage point to become the second American Idol—the two amateur pop singers, both 25, should have been as chilly to each other as Bush and Gore. Instead, the rivals embraced, went on the *AI* tour together and even made plans to do a movie (as had '02 predecessors Kelly Clarkson and Justin Guarini). An Alabama native weighing in at some 360 lbs., Studdard was hailed by Jay Leno as "the sumo of soul." A former music-ed major at Alabama A&M University, Aiken declared, "I'm on a new fork in the road." One with some happy twists. His summer hit "This Is the Night" became one of the year's biggest-selling singles. But he refused to crow, and the competing idols did not become dueling egos. He and Studdard are "very supportive of each other," said Aiken. "He's a friend of mine, plain and simple."

A TABLOID TIZZY

The Mail ON SUNDAY

SUNDAY NEWSPAPER OF THE YEAR

WORLD EXCLUSIVE

CHARLES AND HIS VALET: THE TRUE STORY

By Paul Henderson and David Rowan

Continued on Page 2

Daily Mail

THE PERFECT PRESENT

FREE WEDGWOOD 2003 CALENDAR PLATE WORTH £25 FOR EVERY READER

TOKEN COLLECT PAGE 62

Sensational development as Charles's aide denies rape

PANIC GRIPS THE PALACE

By Richard Kay and Michael Seamark

Daily Mail

NEWSPAPER OF THE YEAR

ELVIS TEN SMASH HITS

FREE INSIDE ELVIS CD

Heartbreak Hotel
Suspicious Minds
Can't Help Falling In Love
Love me Tender
Burning Love
And many more!

INSIDE WEEKEND MAGAZINE

Crisis grows over 'what the servant saw'

CHARLES ON THE RACK

By Richard Kay and Michael Seamark

SOHAM: How the girls died

THE Sun

FRANCE FOR £1

28-PAGE goals Britain's biggest football pullout

ROYALS IN TORMENT

Charles' moment of truth

SOPHIE: IT WAS LIFE OR DEATH

# Prince Charles

## JUST AS CAMILLA AND HE WERE SETTLING IN TOGETHER, THE LONDON PAPERS WERE ABLAZE WITH SALACIOUS SPECULATION

Things seemed to be going so well for Prince Charles, 55. In August, his long-time love, Camilla Parker Bowles, 56, moved in with him at Clarence House, his official London residence, signaling her acceptance by the Queen. Three months later, though, the couple faced a lurid tabloid insinuation: "Is Charles Bisexual?" The innuendo stemmed from an '02 interview in which Charles's ex-valet George Smith claimed he had seen "a member of the royal family" in a compromising situation with a palace servant. *The Mail on Sunday* was ready to ID Charles as the royal in question—until barred by a court injunction. Though the story was widely challenged, Charles's office felt compelled to issue a denial: "The incident which the former employee claims to have witnessed did not take place."

# Colin Farrell

## HOLLYWOOD'S FAVORITE BAD BOY KEEPS NABBING GOOD FILM ROLES

Sometimes it seems as if every sentence out of Farrell's mouth contains the F-word. As in: "I know I'm a fairly f---ing affable bloke and all, but that doesn't always equal charm or a ticket into a woman's pants." In fact, the Irish actor, 27, has charmed plenty of women, including Britney Spears, with whom he was caught smooching on an L.A. hotel balcony in February, and Kim Bordenave, 33, a model with whom he had a son, James, in September. So how does the bloke have time to make movies? In 2003 alone he turned up in five, among them *The Recruit, Phone Booth* (for which he won raves as a man trapped by a sniper), *Daredevil* and *Veronica Guerin.* By year's end he was in Morocco, sweating profusely and profanely over the challenge of playing Alexander the Great. "Me and the lads are trying to ride a horse," he said, "and not look like a bunch of f---ing gimps."

# Mel Gibson

## HIS RAW FILM DEPICTION OF THE CRUCIFIXION STIRRED PRERELEASE CONTROVERSY

Gibson, the Oscar-winning actor-director-producer of *Braveheart,* is known for throwing himself into his films, and *The Passion of the Christ* was no exception. The title, of course, refers to Jesus' last agonizing hours on earth, from his arrest to his death on the cross—which Gibson, 47, captured in excruciating detail. James Caviezel is cast as Christ, and most of the dialogue is in ancient Latin and Aramaic. *The Passion* also speaks to Gibson's fervor in pursuing the $25 million project, which he, a member of the traditionalist Catholic movement, funded himself. Months before its release (slated for Ash Wednesday, 2004), Gibson previewed it in private screenings—triggering an angry debate over what some charged was the film's anti-Semitic tone, holding the Jews responsible for the Crucifixion. Gibson heatedly denied the charge. In response to one attacker, *The New York Times's* Frank Rich, the director told *The New Yorker* magazine, "I want to kill him. I want his intestines on a stick. . . . I want to kill his dog." Now *that's* passion.

"The biggest thing about celebrity is that you just put yourself out there"

# Britney Spears

## THE EX-TEEN QUEEN FLAUNTED A SEXY NEW IMAGE

Can a 22-year-old pop princess (and former Mouseketeer) remake herself into a sexy adult star? In 2003 it wasn't for want of trying. Consider: In January, Spears strode onto a Milan runway modeling a $23,000 rainbow-spangled gown by Donatella Versace. In February, she was spotted canoodling in L.A. with actor Colin Farrell. In April, she shocked fans when she got her hair styled in a brunette chin-length do. In July, she told *W* magazine she was no longer a virgin; her ex, Justin Timberlake, had deflowered her. In August, she shared a deep-tongue kiss with Madonna at the MTV Video Music Awards. (Earlier that month, she was seen cozying up to actor Jared Leto and then sharing a smooch with her choreographer Columbus Short at a rehearsal studio. Oops—he's married. "They're just friends," said her publicist.) In October, while clubbing in Las Vegas, "she was grinding on another girl," said an observer. "It seemed intentionally aimed at shock value." In November, her fourth album, *Get in the Zone,* was released, with songs celebrating Spears's sex drive and the joys of "make-up sex." Was Britney, perhaps, overselling it? Kendel Ehrlich, the wife of Maryland's governor, thought so. "If I had an opportunity to shoot Britney Spears," she said, "I think I would." Oops—just kidding, she later explained.

# Michael Jackson

## CHARGED WITH CHILD MOLESTATION, THE GLOVED (NOW CUFFED) ONE COULD FACE UP TO EIGHT YEARS

With Jackson (who in 2002 dangled his infant son over a hotel balcony), the shocks—if not the hits—keep coming. In a documentary that aired on ABC in February, the eccentric pop star, 45, admitted to having shared his bed with numerous boys but insisted the sleepovers were nonsexual. Fast forward to November, with a handcuffed Jackson being escorted into the Santa Barbara, California, sheriff's office on charges he had committed "lewd or lascivious acts" with a 12-year-old boy. According to reports, the accuser is a cancer patient (now in remission) whose "last wish" had been to meet his idol. The child was said to have revealed that Jackson had plied him with wine before molesting him at Neverland Ranch. Jackson, who posted $3 million bail, called the charges "disgusting" and "totally false." Added his lawyer, Mark Geragos (who was also representing accused wife killer Scott Peterson): "He looks forward to getting into a courtroom and confronting these accusations head-on."

# Roy Horn

**SIEGFRIED'S PARTNER GOT MAULED BY A TIGER, THREATENING HIS LIFE AND DOOMING THEIR ACT**

The admonition "Don't bite the hand that feeds you" evidently mattered not at all to a 600-lb. white tiger named Montecore. Born and bred in captivity, the 7-year-old cat suddenly turned on his master in October, 45 minutes after Horn, 59, and partner Siegfried Fischbacher, 64, had begun their celebrated show at Las Vegas's Mirage hotel. Siegfried later said that Roy had fallen, and speculated that Montecore had tried to help. Whatever set him off, the beast bit into Roy's neck, then exited the stage dragging him by the throat. Montecore released his grip only after being sprayed with a fire extinguisher. Rushed to the hospital, Horn later suffered a massive stroke and was placed on life support. As for Montecore, after a quarantine period, he was allowed to mingle with his two fellow tigers in the Mirage's private zoo. Their performing days may be over, however: Siegfried & Roy's 13-year-old act was suspended indefinitely.

# The Olsen Twins

## FROM TYKES TO TYCOONS, THEY DOUBLE-MINTED A TIDY BUNDLE AND ONE GOT A BOYFRIEND

Okay, here's your handy guide to telling the 5′2″ Ashley (she's on the left) apart from her 5′1″ sister, Mary-Kate. *Clothes:* "I care more about my outfits," said Ashley. "I like mixing vintage with classic pieces." She also "does the shopping for both of us," said Mary-Kate, who called her own fashion tastes "funky. Maybe I'd wear stripes and polka dots, and she'd wear stripes with stripes." *Exercise regimen:* Ashley is into Pilates; Mary-Kate favors power yoga. *Cars:* Ashley drives a green Range Rover; Mary-Kate's RR is black. *Boyfriend:* That would be Ashley's, Matt Kaplan, 19, a Columbia University quarterback. Oh, and did we forget? Ashley is the one with the freckle below her nose. It's the similarities, of course, that matter most. The 17-year-old tycoons—who first charmed us as toddlers on ABC's *Full House* in 1987 and were two of PEOPLE's Most Beautiful People in 2003—are each worth an estimated $150 million, much of it from books, beauty products, electronic games, bedsheets and dolls second only to Barbie in popularity. Don't look for the girls to part company any time soon. Both want to costar in feature films and attend an East Coast college together—one, presumably, that allows Range Rovers on campus.

# The Fab 5

## *QUEER EYE*'S MAKEOVER MAVENS GO INTO THE CLOSET

They arrived each week in a black SUV (with a "FAB 5" vanity plate). Their mission impossible: to remake a hopelessly disheveled hetero bachelor into an impeccably coiffed and outfitted gourmet chef/babe magnet. No way, you say? All in a day's work for the *Queer Eye for the Straight Guy* mavens, who were an immediate summer sensation on cable's Bravo network. The quintet's antic enthusiasm and savvy advice earned them a cult following, repeat showings on NBC and renewal in the fall season. Flamboyant stylist Carson Kressley, 33 (waving the gay pride flag—*yoo*-hoo!), led the pack with his sly put-downs; he was joined by (from left) grooming guru Kyan Douglas, 33 (exfoliate once a week, he advised), interior designer Thom Filicia, 34 (yes, the straight guys' underwear-strewn hovels also required mega renovation), culinary master Ted Allen, 38 (his top tip: use a kitchen blowtorch for browning food), and culture expert Jai Rodriguez, 24. Meanwhile, something else was being rehabbed here: straights' perceptions of gays. *Will & Grace* started it; Carson Kressley & Co. further bridged the gap.

"Have you ever had a man undress you before?"

—CARSON KRESSLEY
TO STRAIGHT-GUY CLIENT BUTCH SCHEPEL

# Nicky & Paris Hilton

### THE IN-CROWD'S TERRIBLE TWOSOME HAD A TRAUMATIC YEAR

"They're beautiful girls who want to have fun," said their great-aunt Francesca of hotel heiresses Paris (right), 22, and Nicky, 20. Maybe too much fun. Paris, a model, had just broken up with fellow mannequin Jason Shaw, and Nicky, a handbag designer, had split with ex-MTV veejay Brian McFayden. Paris diverted herself plugging her upcoming FOX reality series *The Simple Life,* in which she suffered culture shock in an Arkansas farmhouse with actress pal Nicole Richie (Lionel's daughter). Then in November, a mortifying old video surfaced of Paris in an explicit romp with Internet entrepreneur Rick Solomon (who was later married to Shannen Doherty). By then the sisters had taken their tabloid-titillating act to Australia, and the Hilton family issued a statement declaring that they were "greatly saddened at how low human beings will stoop to exploit Paris."

# Lisa Marie Presley

### THE KING'S DAUGHTER RELEASED HER FIRST ALBUM AND KEPT COOL WITH ONE EX

In April, her first CD evoked the inevitable comparisons between Elvis and his 35-year-old daughter. Yes, she had the same pouty lips and hooded eyes, but could she sing like the King? "Gritty, edgy, moody" is how a producer friend described her music, while curious fans propelled *To Whom It May Concern* to No. 5 on Billboard's Top 200 chart its first week in release. Presley, with an estimated net worth of $150 million, didn't seem too concerned about flopping. "I'm not trying to be anything other than myself," said the singer, who dotes on Danielle, 14, and Benjamin, 11, her children by Danny Keough, the first of her three husbands. Presley called her quickie second marriage to Michael Jackson in 1994 a mistake. As for No. 3, Nicolas Cage, they filed for divorce in '02 but continued to socialize. "We're very good friends," she said.

# 50 Cent

## THIS GANSGTA RAPPER HAS STREET CRED: HIS NINE BULLET WOUNDS

There is no real plan B for the rapper born Curtis Jackson 27 years ago in the New York borough of Queens. "If it doesn't work for me musically, then I go back to the street," he said, "which is going back to nothing." The thuggish ex-con turned gangsta rapper ought to know. His mother, a crack dealer, was killed when he was 8, and in 2000 he survived nine gunshot wounds likely fired by a rival hip-hop group. His fledgling career also suffered a hit after the attack but was revived thanks to the support of fans like Dr. Dre and Eminem, who featured 50 Cent on the soundtrack of his '02 movie *8 Mile*. Since then, 50 Cent's album *Get Rich or Die Tryin'* has gone platinum, and he became partners in the G-Unit clothing line that works his name into every price tag—e.g., not \$29 but \$29.50 for a signature T-shirt. Nowadays, determined to avoid the fate of murdered rappers like his idol, Tupac Shakur, 50 Cent wears a bulletproof vest and only rides in a bulletproof car.

# Reese Witherspoon

**ON THE SET OF HER NEXT FLICK, THE STAR PROVED SHE WAS A WORKING MOM-TO-BE**

When you see Witherspoon, 27, as a pregnant Becky Sharp in the latest film version of *Vanity Fair,* that's not just padding: The actress was in fact carrying Deacon, her second child with actor husband Ryan Phillippe, 29. Daughter Ava, 4, "will be a great older sister," predicted Witherspoon, who gave birth October 23. Productive otherwise too, she also delivered with the sequel *Legally Blonde 2.* Reprising that ditzy lawyer role earned another $15 million for Hollywood's most bankable star under 30. First and foremost, though, "I'm a mom and a wife," she insisted. "And that's what I like to be."

# The Newlyweds

## NICK LACHEY AND JESSICA SIMPSON LET CAMERAS EAVESDROP—FOR BETTER *AND* FOR WORSE

Perhaps their October 2002 nuptials should have contained a clause like this: "Do you, Jessica, and you, Nick, promise to allow a film crew into your house to record your every waking and (almost) every intimate moment for the first five months of your marriage?" Well, they did, they did. And viewers of the series *Newlyweds: Nick & Jessica* got to see pop star Simpson, 23, and ex-98° frontman Lachey, 30, squabble over everything from finances to laundry. We also heard Simpson ask, "Where do buffalo wings come from? Chickens or buffaloes?"—along with other addled musings that would make another Simpson—Homer—slap his forehead. The loopiness made the show a regular target on ABC's *Jimmy Kimmel Live* but proved a ratings magnet for the desirable 12-34 demographic. As a result, MTV happily renewed *Newlyweds* for a second season. As Homer Simpson might say: *D'oh!*

# Reality Couples

## TV PLAYED CUPID, BUT ONLY ONE DUO WAS READY TO WED

### Trista and Ryan

Since their courtship was played out in front of a national audience—on ABC's *The Bachelorette*—it was only fitting that the nuptials of Rehn, 31, and her firefighter beau, Sutter (far left), 29, be televised too. The first of the reality-show singles to tie the knot, they set up house near Vail, Colorado, weeks before the big day. Though they seemed cozy together, the couple had another powerful incentive to wed: a $1 million fee from ABC. I do, *ka-ching?* "If you don't want to believe in us, that's okay," said Rehn, an aspiring TV personality. "We're still going to be in love."

### Andrew and Jen

In contrast to Trista and Ryan, millionaire vintner Firestone, 28, and Schefft, 27, the Chicago account exec he proposed to in May on *The Bachelor,* ABC's original singles cattle call, said they were in no hurry to wed and had no intention of letting the network tape any ceremony. A further indication of their tenuousness: Though Schefft moved into Firestone's two-bedroom San Francisco apartment, his insurance-salesman roommate did not move out. When the couple broke up after 10 months, Andrew stated that they were "totally amicable" but "our future goals are different."

# Queen Latifah

## THERE WAS LESS OF HER THANKS TO BREAST REDUCTION, BUT HER PERSONALITY REMAINED EXUBERANTLY PLUS-SIZE

In her Oscar-nominated portrayal of a brassy prison matron in 2002's *Chicago* and her hilarious turn as the funky escaped convict who wins Steve Martin's heart in the 2003 hit *Bringing Down the House,* Latifah, 33, used her full figure to full advantage. But "her chest has always caused her back pain," said her rep, explaining why she underwent breast-reduction surgery this year. In addition, she shed more than 25 lbs. through diet and a regimen of kickboxing and hiking. The result: "It's easier for clothes to fit," said stylist Susan Moses. "But then, when you're the Queen, they will make adjustments. Her focus isn't to be a waif." Indeed not, said Latifah. "I'm cool with myself. If I can't have the body of Angie Bassett, so be it." Certainly her self-confidence hasn't shrunk. As Phillip Noyce, her director in 1999's *The Bone Collector,* put it: "She has a big aura. She owns every room she's in."

# *Friends*

## THEY WERE THERE FOR US—NOW IT'S BYE-BYE

I can't even think about it. I get anxiety," said Jennifer Aniston (Rachel, bottom right), 34, pondering the 10th and final season of TV's hottest sitcom. "It's like a divorce nobody wants." By the fall of '03, nobody seemed to know for sure how it would all end in May '04. Would Ross and Rachel make up? Would Chandler and Monica make a baby? "I know that we want all the characters to be happy, hopefully," said Lisa Kudrow (Phoebe, bottom middle), 40. While their characters fussed and feuded, dated, mated, divorced and had babies, the *Friends* cast formed genuine friendships offscreen, attending each other's premieres and weddings. "There's never once in 10 years been a raised voice here," said Matthew Perry (Chandler, top right), 34. But now the show was overshadowing all of them. "It's bittersweet," said David Schwimmer (Ross, bottom left), 37, of the upcoming final filming in January. "We're definitely going to be feeling some sadness." For Courteney Cox (Monica, top middle), 39, life after *Friends* is "going to be a killer. I mean, these are my buds." At least Matt LeBlanc (Joey, top left), 36, had reason to smile: His character has been promised a spinoff series. NBC's accountants were also elated: The *Friends* finale will ring up $2 million per 30-second spot.

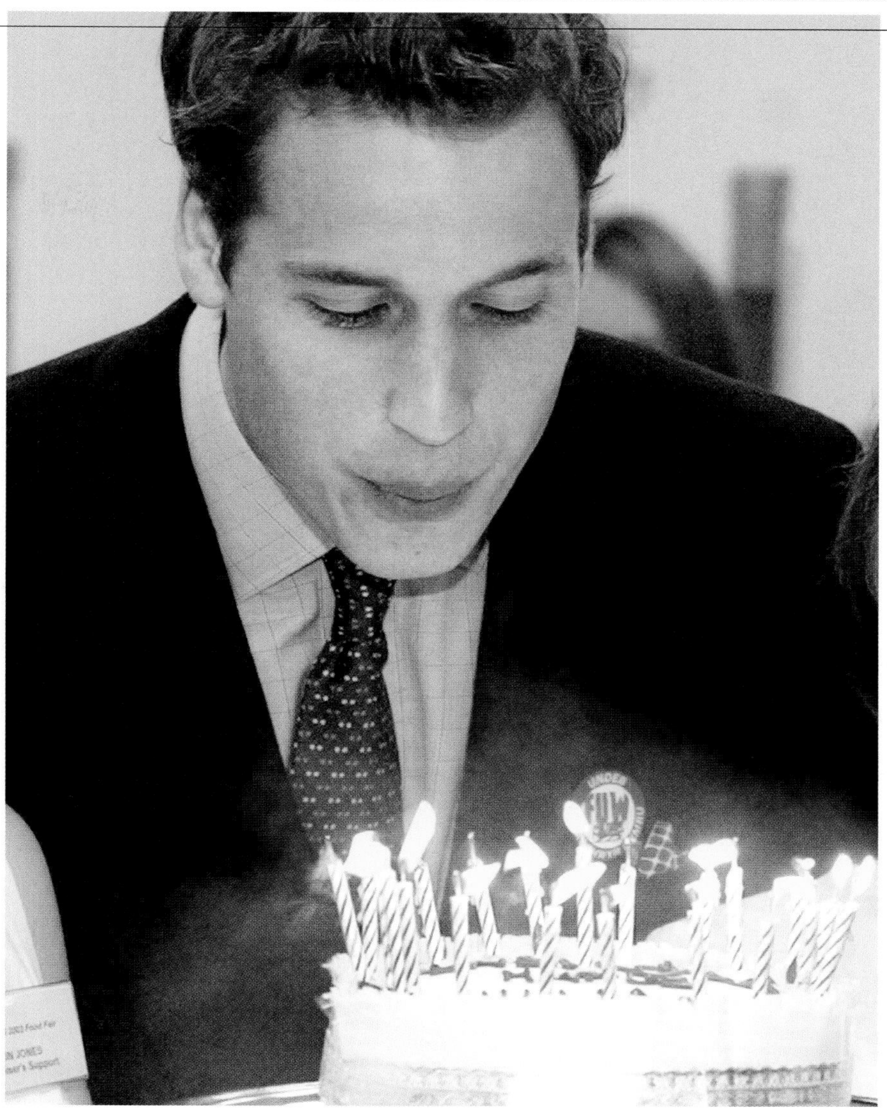

# Prince William

## POLO, ANYONE? HAVING TURNED 21, THE WINDSOR HEIR THREW HIMSELF INTO RIDING, SCOTTISH DANCING AND FLIRTING

On June 21, the young man who would be king celebrated his 21st birthday with an "Out of Africa" theme party at Windsor Castle. He dressed as a bush tribesman; his dad, Prince Charles, wore a flowing striped caftan. In 2001, Wills visited Kenya, where he befriended Jessica Craig, daughter of a game-preserve owner. Though she was among the birthday guests, insiders deny they are romantically linked; nor is he more than "just friends" with another guest, Kate Middleton, a former roomie at the University of St. Andrews in Scotland. The prince, a junior, is majoring in art history and currently living off campus in a farmhouse. "I don't have a girlfriend," he said in a pre-birthday interview. "[But] if I fancy a girl and she fancies me . . . I ask her out." One warning for his dates: "I love Scottish dancing," said William. "I do throw my arms dangerously around, and girls fly across the dance floor." He is possibly safer in the saddle of a polo pony; William, Dad and brother Harry, 19, an Eton College grad, are all avid players. "He's having the time of his life," noted royal-watch writer Brian Hoey. William is also "sensible and very well-balanced for his age," added a family friend. And mindful of his destiny. "He has come to terms," said British journalist Peter Archer, "with the thought that one day he will be king."

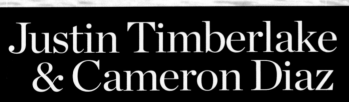

# Justin Timberlake & Cameron Diaz

**JUDGING BY THEIR DISPLAYS OF AFFECTION, THE ANGEL AND THE SINGER WERE DEFINITELY IN SYNC**

Since they began dating in April, Timberlake, 22, in recovery from Britney Spears, and Diaz, 31, coming off a four-year relationship with actor-musician Jared Leto, have been dramatically and publicly "demonstrative" together. Or that's how one witness described their embraces at a party following the 'N Sync heartthrob's guest-host stint on *Saturday Night Live* in October. A month earlier, they were spotted kissing throughout a sushi dinner at a Honolulu restaurant. And during one of his August gigs, the ebullient *Charlie's Angels* star had sung along from the audience while holding hands with Timberlake's mom, Lynn Harless. On another occasion at a Chicago eatery, a customer complained to the manager, "They're too loud. Can you get them to shut up?" Overhearing that, Diaz let loose another laugh. "Justin," reported a family insider, "said she's a lot of fun."

"You're not waiting for a punch line with her. You're just waiting for her to speak so you can start laughing"

—*NEMO* DIRECTOR ANDREW STANTON

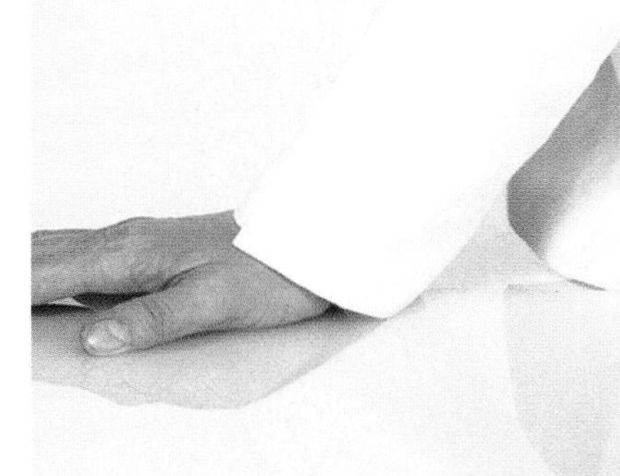

# Ellen DeGeneres

## TALK ABOUT VERSATILE: ELLEN SCORED AS A FISH, AN AUTHOR AND THE NEW QUEEN OF NICE

Things went swimmingly this year for DeGeneres, 45—starting with her acclaimed voice-over role as Dory, the chatterbox regal blue tang fish, in the animated summer smash *Finding Nemo*. Then, in September, the wry stand-up turned sitcom headliner (*Ellen*) found her niche as a daytime doyenne on the syndicated *Ellen DeGeneres Show,* charming critics and snaring ratings with her low-key banter. Her wit was also on display in *The Funny Thing Is . . .*, her second collection of comic essays. On the home front, too, life was good. Actress-photographer Alexandra Hedison, 34, her girlfriend of three years, "is the perfect partner for Ellen," raved pal Melissa Etheridge. "They're very, very in love." Might there be an addition? "I can't imagine not at some point having a child," said DeGeneres.

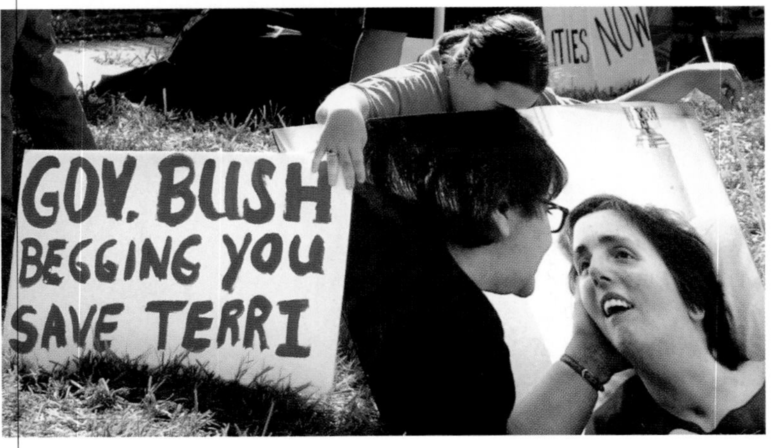


# Terri Schiavo

### FLORIDA'S GOVERNOR STEPPED INTO A FAMILY FEUD INVOLVING A LIFE-OR-DEATH DECISION

In a vegetative state since suffering a heart attack 13 years ago, Schiavo, 40, was caught in a bitter battle between her husband, Michael, who since 1998 has sought to remove her feeding tube, and her parents, Robert and Mary Schindler, who wanted her kept alive. In October, Florida governor Jeb Bush, backed by the state legislature, interceded for the parents, sparking more controversy and guaranteeing a prolonged court battle.

# Kirk Jones

### THIS DAREDEVIL TOOK THE ULTIMATE PLUNGE

In October, Jones, 41, an unemployed Canton, Michigan, man, went over the top—of Niagara Falls, that is—and survived, the first person in history to do so without benefit of barrel or any safety device. The police who arrested Jones would no doubt agree with his proposed book title: *You're Kidding Me: A Knucklehead's Guide to Surviving Niagara Falls.*

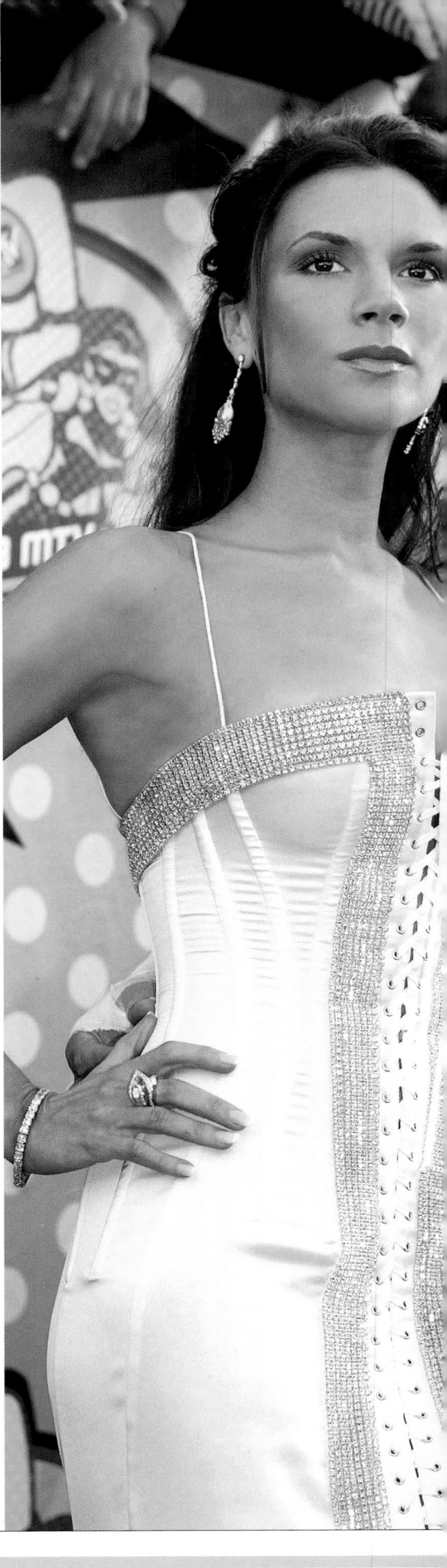

# The Beckhams

## HIS EYE'S ON THE BALL, SHE'S INTO MUSIC: IS THERE DISHARMONY?

To the English, they were entertainment royalty; their 24-acre spread outside London was dubbed Beckingham Palace. But in June, David, 28, the world's highest-paid soccer player, signed with the Real Madrid team, for which he was to earn nearly $30 million in salary and endorsements, and by fall there were rumors of a rift between him and wife Victoria, 29, former Spice Girl "Posh" Adams. She reportedly resented their uprooting to Madrid with sons Brooklyn, 4, and Romeo, 1, and he hated her being away in New York, where she was working on a comeback album. Then, to bend it like Beckham, the couple issued a joint statement: "Our marriage is not in trouble. We are very much enjoying our new life in Spain."

# Aron Ralston

## FACING A CRUEL CHOICE BETWEEN LIFE AND LIMB, THIS HIKER OPTED TO SURVIVE

It was like a chapter out of those *Worst Case Scenario* guides: Ralston, 28, an Aspen, Colorado, man, was hiking alone in a remote Utah canyon in April when an 800-lb. boulder he'd stepped onto suddenly shifted, pinning him by his right arm. For the next six days, Ralston lay trapped, scraping futilely at the boulder with his knife. Dehydrated and without food, "I thought I was going to die," he said. Finally, he decided instead to turn the blade on his arm, hacking through bone, tendons and nerves despite the excruciating pain. His self-amputation completed, he applied a tourniquet, then managed to rappel 60 feet down a cliff and walk six miles before finding help. Five operations later, Ralston wears a prosthesis—one customized for rock climbing. "I'm certainly more aware of the risks involved in the things I like to do," he observed. "If I decide to stray from the path, I think about it first."

# Hillary Clinton

SHE SCORED AN UNEXPECTED BESTSELLER, AND EVEN FOES OF THE FAMILY CONCEDED THAT SHE HAD MADE HERSELF AT HOME ON THE HILL—AND THE HIGH WIRE

America's polarized feelings about her husband hardly slowed the former First Lady, 56, now junior senator from New York. Tirelessly cultivating her constituents and deferring to senior Senate colleagues, she was hailed as "the perfect student" by West Virginia veteran Robert Byrd. "She's more of a star than the other 99 of us combined," said another Democrat, Minnesota's Mark Dayton. Indeed, her memoir, *Living History,* shot to the top of the charts in June, eventually selling more than 1.4 million copies. In it she recalled "crying and yelling" at Bill when he belatedly confessed to lying about Monica Lewinsky; it was, she wrote, "the most hurtful experience of my life." But, otherwise, the book read as cautiously as a campaign biography, and there was speculation that she might vie for the White House as early as '04. "I'm having the time of my life," she told Homeland Security official Asa Hutchinson, an ex-congressman who served as a manager at her husband's impeachment trial. "I pinch myself every morning."

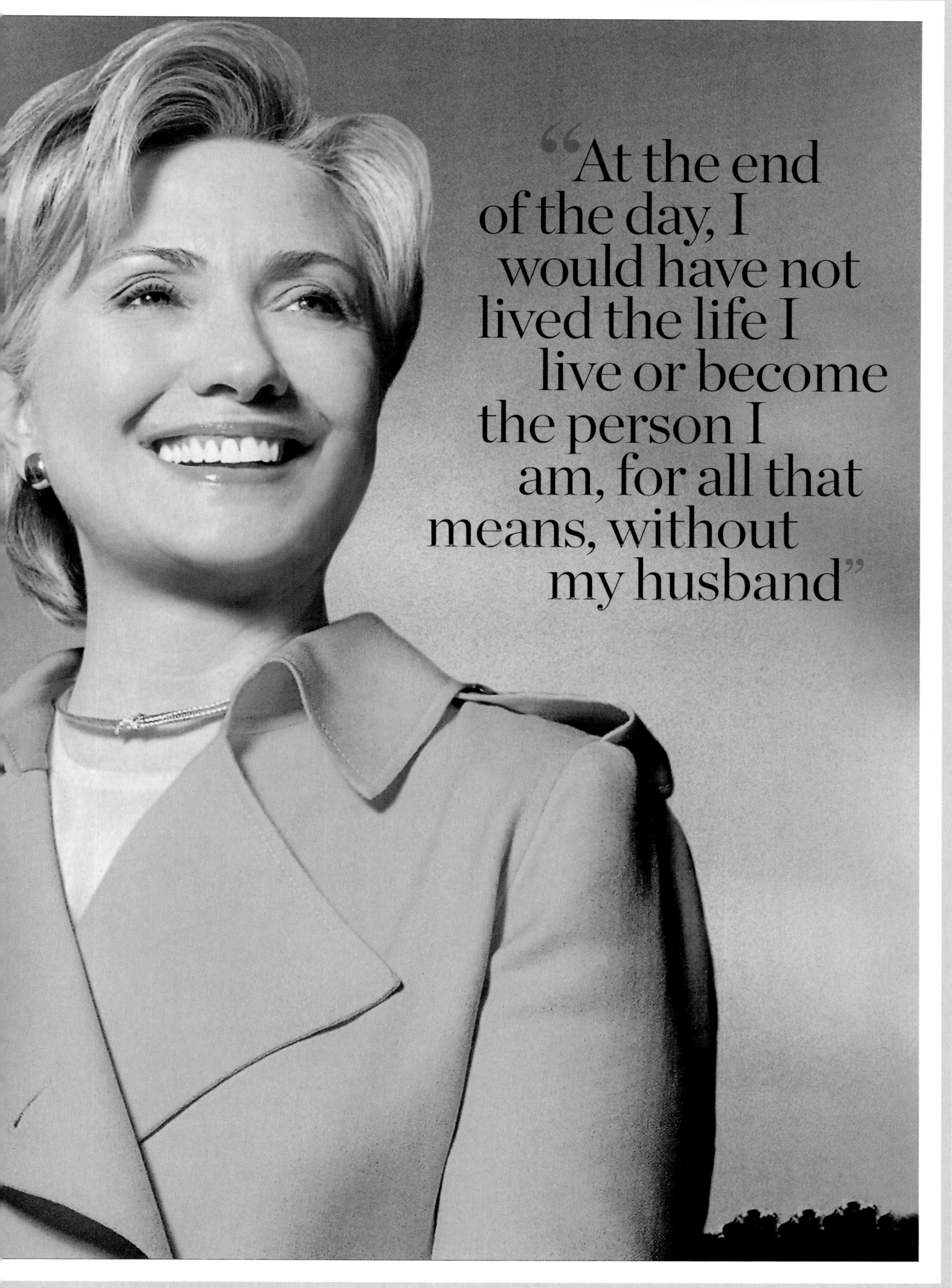
"At the end
of the day, I
would have not
lived the life I
live or become
the person I
am, for all that
means, without
my husband"

# Hilary Duff

## TELEVISION'S TWEEN TITAN MADE THE BIG LEAP TO MOVIES, MUSIC, HER OWN FASHION LABEL AND *CINDERELLA*

Fame is "so, like, unreal to me," said the teen star of TV's *Lizzie McGuire*, "'cause I'm really a normal kid." That quality may explain the popularity of the Texas-born actress on the small screen (*Lizzie* ruled as the top-rated show for kids 9 to 14, and Duff nabbed a CBS sitcom development deal) and the large (*The Lizzie McGuire Movie*). Now, "I want to move on," said Duff, who at 16 released her first solo album, launched her own funky fashion line and a forthcoming prepaid Duff Visa Card—and signed for a reported $2 million to star in a new film version of *Cinderella*. Like her fairy-tale character, Duff is seeking her prince, having been flirtatiously on-again, off-again with a fellow 16-year-old, singer Aaron Carter.

# Gay Marriage

## WEDDING BELLS RANG FOR GAYS IN CANADA. COULD THE U.S. BE NEXT?

Tom Graff (left), 58, and Anthony Porcino, 35, wasted no time. Just an hour after an appeals court made British Columbia the second Canadian province to allow same-sex marriage, the Vancouver pair (partners for 11 years) became the first gay couple to exchange vows legally in B.C. South of the border, too, same-sex unions made strides. In June, the Supreme Court struck down a Texas law banning sodomy between consenting homosexual adults. In California and other states, gay-rights activists lobbied for a law similar to Vermont's, which grants child custody and other marital rights to same-sex couples who wed in a civil ceremony there. In November, the Massachusetts supreme court ruled that its legislature could approve gay marriage. But the cause also had its opponents, most notably Pope John Paul II and President Bush, who declared, "I believe marriage is between a man and a woman."

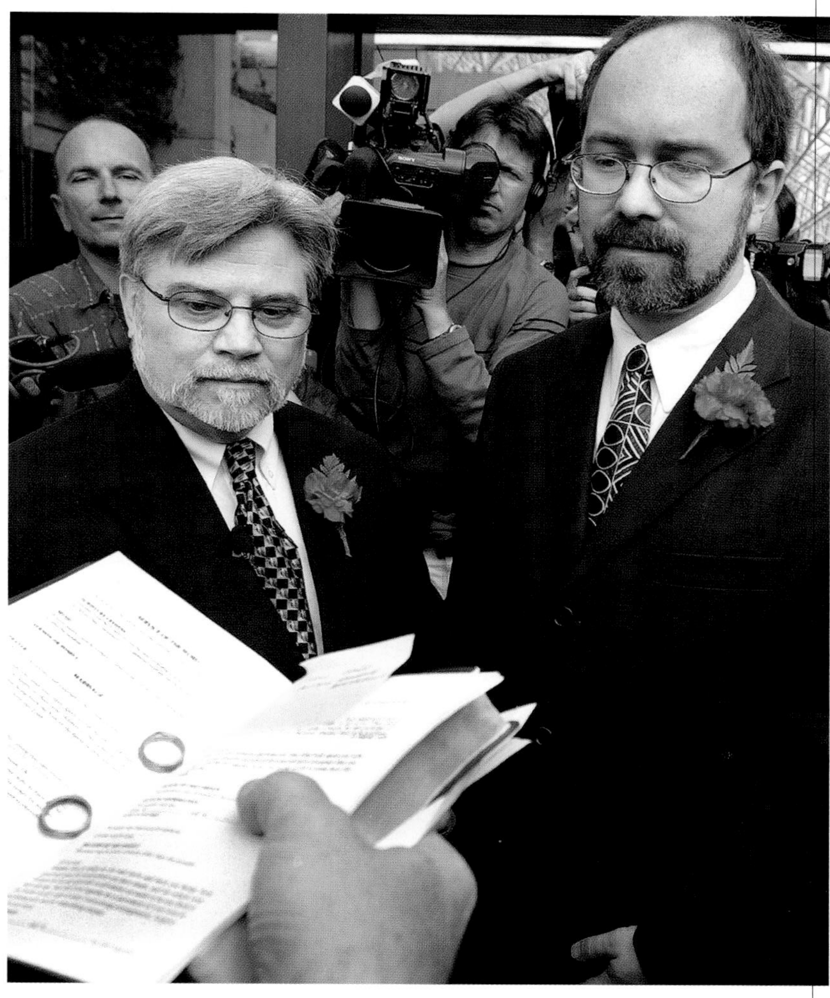

# Gary Ridgway

## CONFESSING TO 48 MURDERS, THE 'GREEN RIVER' SERIAL KILLER CHEATED DEATH

"I killed so many women, I had a hard time keeping them straight." With those chilling words, Ridgway, 54, a commercial truck painter, pled guilty in a Seattle courtroom in November to murdering 48 women—many of them prostitutes and runaways—from approximately 1982 to 1984 in the Pacific Northwest. A suspect since 1983, Ridgway may have subsequently killed a dozen more before he was finally nailed by DNA evidence and a county sheriff, Dave Reichert, who toiled 21 years on the case. Through his plea bargain, Ridgway was able to avoid the death penalty. Though the district attorney said he had agonized over the deal that gave closure to the worst serial-killing spree in U.S. history, many victims' survivors were outraged. Summed up one: "I want him dead."

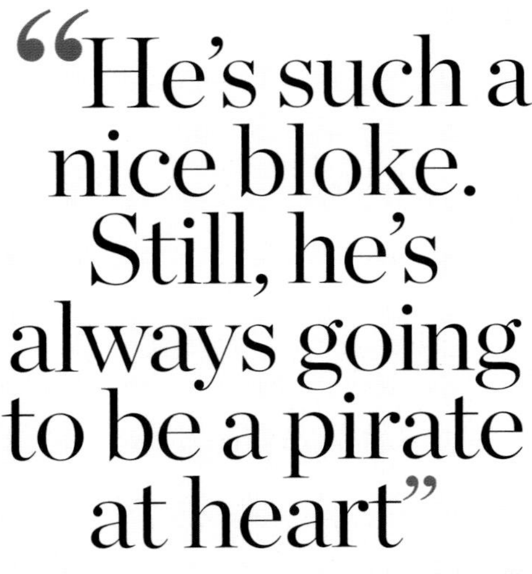

"He's such a nice bloke. Still, he's always going to be a pirate at heart"

—*CARIBBEAN* COSTAR KEIRA KNIGHTLEY

# Johnny Depp

**ARRGH! THE ACCLAIMED MOVIE PIRATE TURNED WAR CRITIC WENT OUT ON A PLANK**

From mutant topiary artist Edward Scissorhands to Z-movie director Ed Wood, Johnny Depp, 40, has never shied from outlandish roles. But his bravura portrayal of the fey, flighty yet fiercely gallant Jack Sparrow in Disney's summer hit *Pirates of the Caribbean: The Curse of the Black Pearl* may be the most popular performance of his iconoclastic career. "There's no b.s., no attitude," said his *Pirates* director Gore Verbinski. "He enjoys acting, and it shows." Depp also loves the expatriate life in France, where he shares a $2 million villa with his actress-singer girlfriend, Vanessa Paradis, 31, and their children Lily-Rose, 4, and Jack, 1. "Each morning I can go to the little village not far from my house, have a cup of coffee, sit there with my girl and not worry about the paparazzi," he said, a relief for PEOPLE's Sexiest Man Alive of 2003. The pastoral escape has not mellowed his politics, though, and he took a harsh view of the invasion of Iraq, telling a German magazine, "America . . . is something like a dumb puppy that has big teeth—that can bite and hurt you." A day later, perhaps trying to extricate foot from mouth, Depp said "there was no anti-American sentiment" in his statement. "I love my country and have great hopes for it," which is why "I speak candidly and sometimes critically about it."

# Paul Burrell

**THE BUTLER DID IT: HIS NEW MEMOIR DISHED ON DI'S TRAVAILS, PROVING A ROYAL PAIN TO HER FAMILY**

Princess Di feared she was targeted for foul play. . . . Prince Philip rebuked both her and Charles for having affairs. . . . Diana's own brother snubbed her. . . . Those were among the bombshells dropped by her longtime butler Burrell, 45, in his memoir *A Royal Duty.* The author called the book "a loving tribute," but Di's son Prince William, speaking for the family, saw it as "a cold and overt betrayal." His mother would have been "mortified" by her servant's blabbing, said William, and he sought a private meeting with Burrell to forestall any further revelations. Burrell, charged in 2002 with stealing Di's keepsakes but acquitted after the Queen spoke up for him, was unrepentant. "My name has been trashed, my family has been put through hell, and I have been on the brink of suicide," he told the BBC. "I am a human being too, and I need to put the record straight."

# Pope John Paul II

## PHYSICALLY AILING YET SPIRITUALLY STRONG, THE PONTIFF MARKED A QUARTER-CENTURY REIGN BY TRAVELING WIDELY AND TACKLING ONE OF THE CHURCH'S THORNIEST PROBLEMS

Despite concerns over his fragile health, the 83-year-old Pontiff pursued a grueling travel schedule that took him to Spain, Croatia, Bosnia and Slovakia in 2003, thus achieving a personal milestone of 100 trips outside Italy. But it was back home in the Vatican where he continued to address one of the Catholic Church's most pressing issues: the scandal of pedophiliac priests. In February, the Pope approved reforms that made it easier to expel offenders from the priesthood. During the year, he also beatified Mother Teresa and installed 31 new cardinals (increasing speculation about which of the 195 "red hats"—all but five handpicked by the theologically conservative John Paul II—would be elected as his successor). Earlier, the native of Wadowice, Poland, celebrated the 25th year of his papacy. The effects of Parkinson's disease, arthritis and other ailments had clearly taken their toll. Addressing pilgrims in St. Peter's Square in October, the Pope had to be wheeled onto the stage and was too weak to read more than portions of his homily. Still, he left many of his listeners inspired. "It's just his presence," said Tim Kennedy, a visitor from Summit, New Jersey. "He's saying don't lose faith, the church is still vibrant, it's not just an artifact, you have to live it every day."

# Shock AND Awe

WE MARVELED AT MARS AND WERE SHAKEN BY SARS. THE RED PLANET MADE ITS CLOSEST APPROACH SINCE THE STONE AGE, WHILE THE EXOTIC DISEASE CAME TOO CLOSE FOR COMFORT. WILDFIRES AND A MONSTER HURRICANE ALSO STRUCK, AND A BEAUTIFUL RARE BIRD CALLED THE SST MADE ITS NOISY FINAL FLIGHT

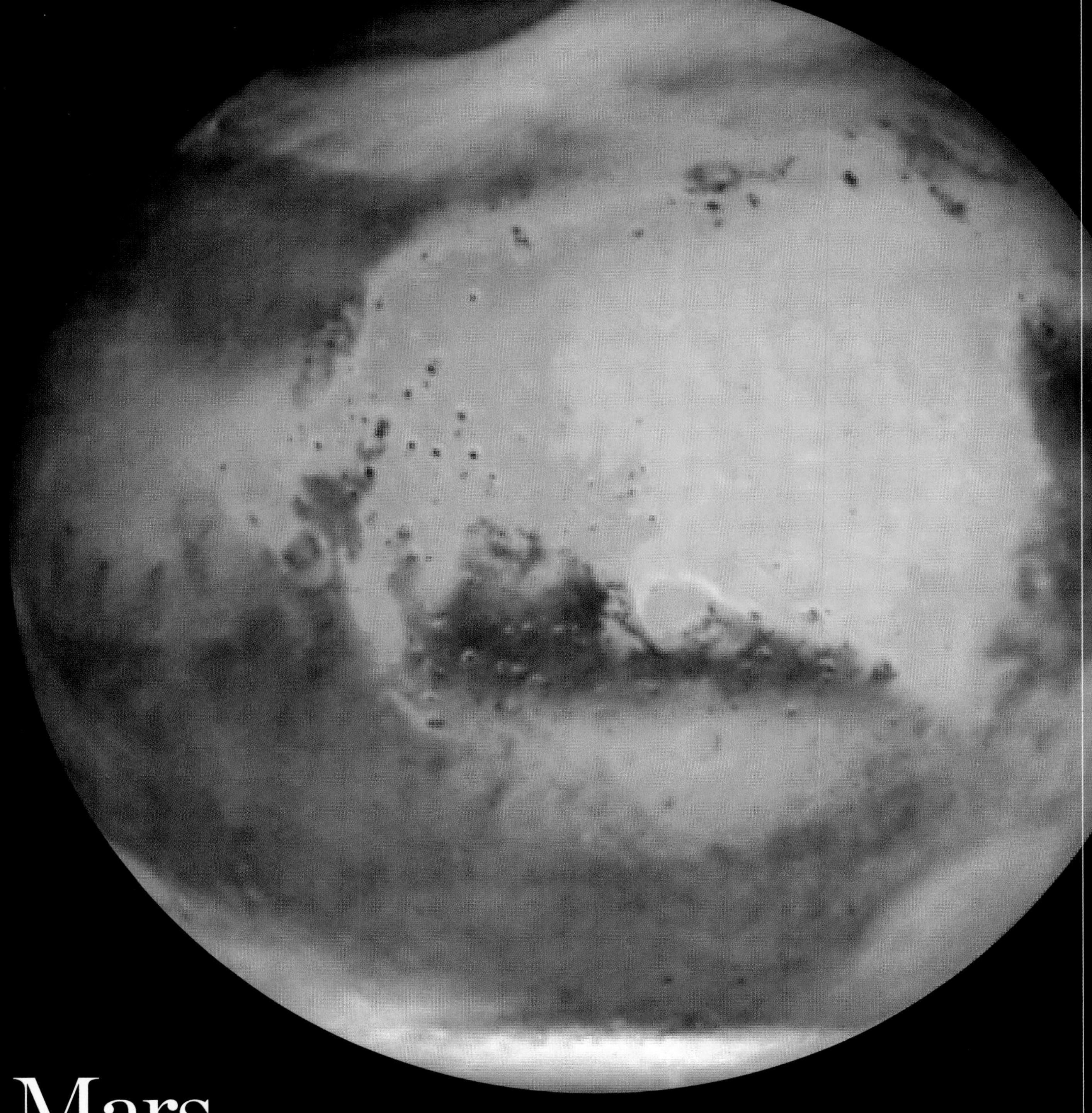

# Mars

## ON ITS CLOSEST PASS IN NEARLY 600 CENTURIES, THE RED PLANET FIRED UP OUR IMAGINATIONS

No, the Martians didn't land and aim their heat rays at us—this time. But they wouldn't have had so far to travel—a mere 34.6 million miles, which is the closest our world has been to the fourth rock from the sun in, oh, 59,619 years. What most of us saw down here in late August was a brilliant reddish-pink glow in the southeastern sky. NASA engineers, meanwhile, had even bolder visions—of us invading *them. Beagle 2,* a 143-lb., European-launched robotic probe named after Charles Darwin's ship, was scheduled to parachute down to the Martian surface around Christmas. A month later, a pair of NASA rovers were expected to start scuttling around. "I guarantee you," said one scientist, "we're going to find new things." A manned landing would cost billions and is undoubtedly decades away. So if that doesn't happen, well, please mark August 28, 2287, on your descendants' calendars. That's when Mars gets even more neighborly—veering 40,000 miles closer than it did in 2003.

# “We watched New York from our roofs, and it was quite beautiful. You never normally see the stars in the city”

–**SARAH COATES,** TEXTILE DESIGNER

# The Blackout

**WHERE WERE *YOU* WHEN THE LIGHTS WENT OUT IN THE EAST? NOT, WE HOPE, ON A ROLLER COASTER, AN ELEVATOR, A SUBWAY OR AN OPERATING-ROOM GURNEY**

It was the monster that devoured Cleveland. Then, in just a few startled blinks of the eye, Detroit, Toronto, New York and most of New England all succumbed to the invisible Godzilla. As night fell on August 14, some 50 million Americans in eight states were left in the dark and forced to cope with the most widespread power outage in U.S. history. Cope they did—often heroically. In New York City, *Lord of the Rings* star Sean Astin joined an emergency-services unit rescuing people trapped in elevators. In Ann Arbor, Michigan, hospital courier Robert Moore, after getting stalled in traffic, hopped a bike to deliver lifesaving blood platelets to a cancer patient. In Massachusetts, stranded roller-coaster riders ("Thank God, not up on top," said one) were eased to earth. The cause of the blackout was disputed, but, guessed Manhattanite Alex Ewen: "Homer Simpson spilled his coffee on the control panel of the Springfield nuclear power plant."

# Hurricane Isabel

SHE HUFFED AND SHE PUFFED, BLOWING ROOFS AND POWER LINES DOWN AND LEAVING CASUALTIES AND A SOGGY MESS ALONG THE EAST COAST

Those aren't the canals of Venice but the submerged streets of Annapolis, Maryland, one of the East Coast cities hardest hit by Isabel in September. *The New York Times* dubbed the storm "an equal-opportunity destroyer." Rich and poor felt her wrath from North Carolina (buffeted by 100-mph winds) through Virginia (which got inundated with 11 inches of rain) to Pennsylvania and New Jersey (where downed power lines left millions in the dark for days afterward). "I've been here since 1985 and seen Hurricane Hugo, Gloria and Andrew," said the owner of a Baltimore bar filled with six feet of river. "Those were class three, four hurricanes, and the water was never as high as this storm."

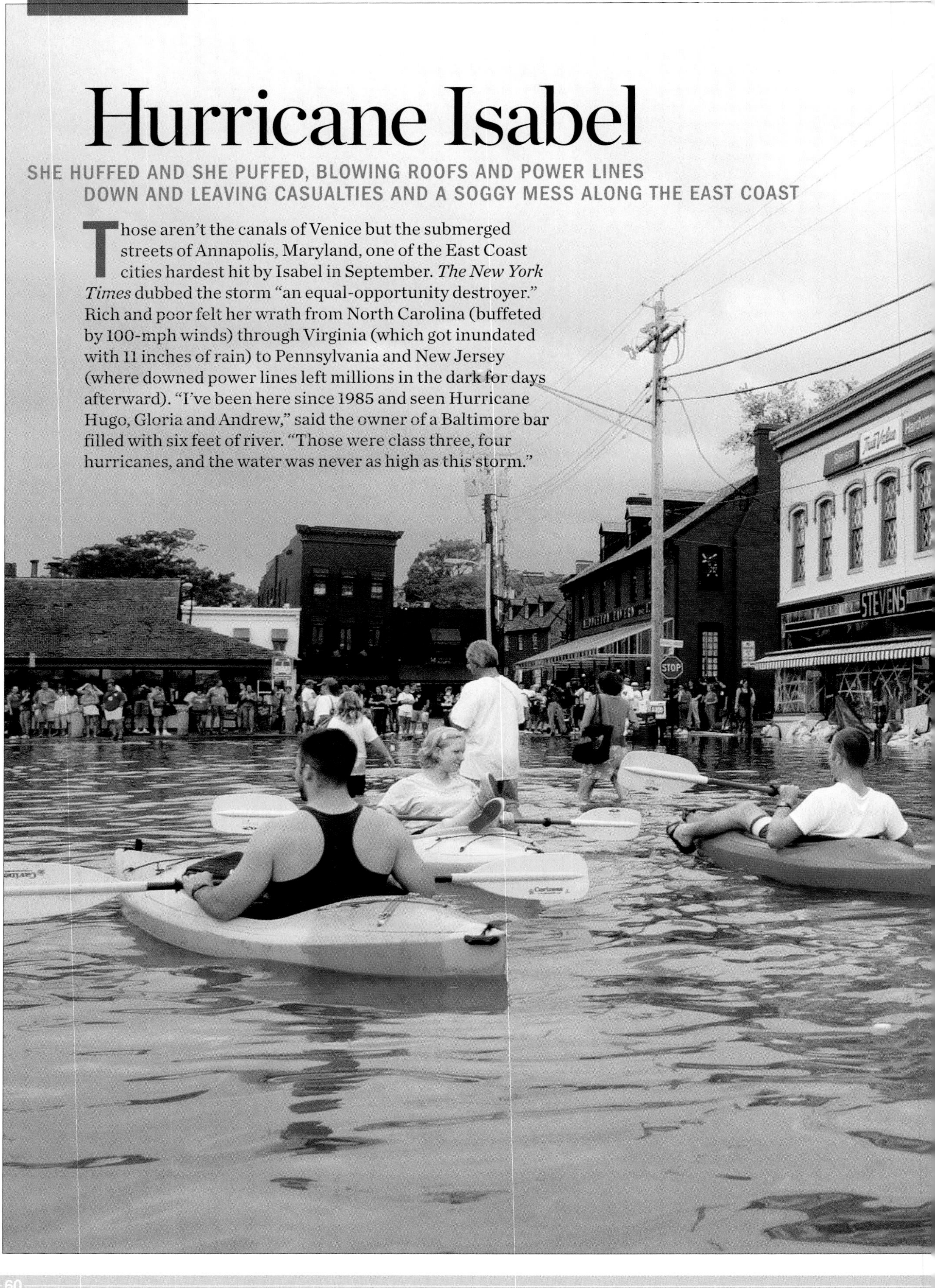

# The *Columbia* Crew

## BEFORE THEY FELL TO EARTH, THE SEVEN ASTRONAUTS HAD FULFILLED THEIR DREAM

Mission commander Rick Husband (front right), 45, would dress up in his spacesuit for Halloween; pilot William McCool (front left), 41, had been one of the best long-distance runners in West Texas. As for their crew, Laurel Clark (middle right), 41, considered being a mom to 8-year-old Iain "my most important job"; Kalpana Chawla (middle left), 41, had talked of going to the moon while in high school in Karnal, India; Ilan Ramon (back left), 48, was a colonel in the Israeli air force; David Brown (back right), 46, a former flight surgeon, was "like a kid in a candy store" as an astronaut, said a friend; and Michael Anderson (back center), 43, was one of only seven active-duty black astronauts in NASA when he and his six *Columbia* shipmates prepared for landing in Houston on February 1. Just after 8 a.m. CST, the space shuttle began to disintegrate at 175,000 feet, raining 234,000 lbs. of debris along a 240-mile-long swath in Texas and Louisiana and killing all seven aboard. An official report blamed NASA administrators for failing to note the significance of postlaunch debris that had struck *Columbia's* wing two weeks earlier, dooming the astronauts on reentry.

# SARS

### FROM CHINA WITH FEAR: A DEADLY NEW VIRUS CAUSED CONCERN WORLDWIDE

For epidemiologists, the world may be getting too small. SARS—a potentially fatal virus traced to porcupines, civet cats, raccoon dogs and other wild animals sold as food in rural China—was unwittingly carried by airline passengers to Toronto. That led to a brief—and protested—travel quarantine for residents of the Canadian city. By May there were almost 5,000 reported cases of SARS in 26 countries, with a fatality rate of 6 percent. The year also saw a smaller, less contagious outbreak of monkeypox, another interspecies illness believed to be transmitted to humans from Gambian rats, prairie dogs and other popular exotic pets. Small wonder that *28 Days Later,* a summer thriller about a chimp-borne epidemic that transmuted meek Londoners into raging zombies, caught fire at the box office. Science fiction? Maybe not, someday.

# The Concorde

### A DREAMY FLIGHT OF FANCY PROVED PERHAPS TOO FANCY TO STAY ALOFT

It was called a "supersonic snobmobile." Indeed, on the British Airways jet's final flight, from New York's JFK to London's Heathrow in October, passengers like Christie Brinkley and broadcaster Sir David Frost were sipping Dom Perignon and dining on lobster truffle salad. The SST, which first took off 27 years ago, was a beauty to behold and an engineering marvel—able to fly at twice the speed of sound, crossing from New York to London in 3¼ hours, to Paris in 3¾. But it was doomed by its impracticality (who else but the rich and famous could afford the $9,300 round trip?), and the aging, money-losing, ear-shattering seven-plane fleet was finally retired. To residents near JFK, the last takeoff was a godsend. Said one: "We needed that noise like we needed a hole in our heads."

# California Wildfires

## SURVIVORS SIGHED (OR CHOKED) IN RELIEF AS RAINS QUENCHED A TOWERING INFERNO

"At first I saw no homes, just chimneys, smoke and flames," said Mike Shambach, 44, a resident of Scripps Ranch, a San Diego suburb. "When I came around our corner, I saw the top of a roof that looked like mine. It was our house. Everything around it was gone or smoldering, but our house wasn't touched at all. No scorch marks, no windows blown out. I was in shock." Shambach and his family were among the lucky few in the path of one of the worst fires in California history to escape with their property unscathed. The windswept conflagrations, believed to be started by arsonists, wiped out more than 3,500 homes and 746,000 acres and caused some two dozen deaths. The disaster also put a further $2 billion dent in the state's staggering economy. The flames, which cast a thick toxic haze over the region, were snuffed out only after the weeks-long efforts of 15,000 firefighters (like Eric Brue, above) working round the clock and a provident turn in the weather: heavy rains and cooler temperatures. "People joke with me and say that when they rebuild, my house is going to be an eyesore," said Shambach. "When you hear joking like that, you know the healing has begun."

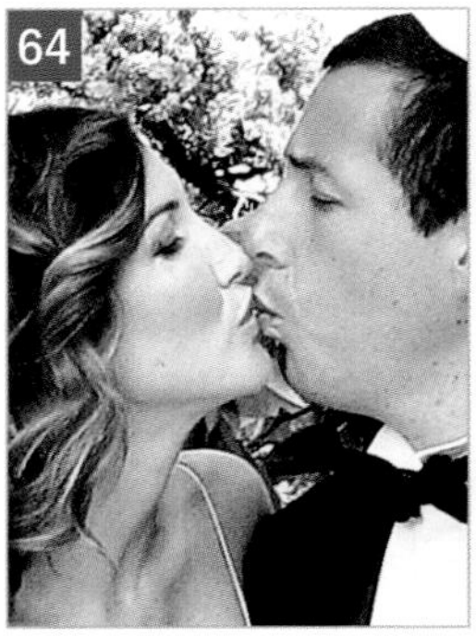


WEDDINGS

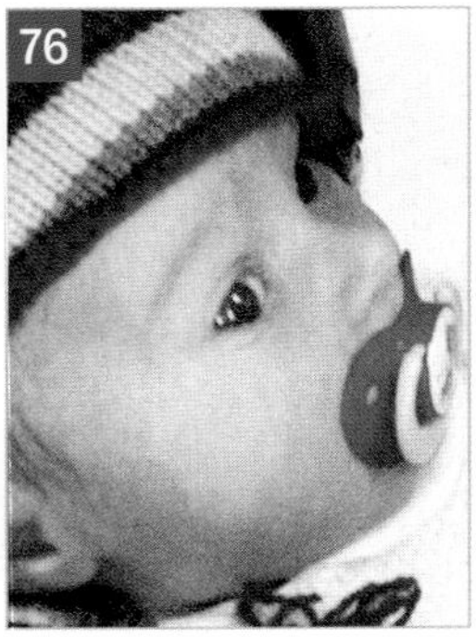


BIRTHS

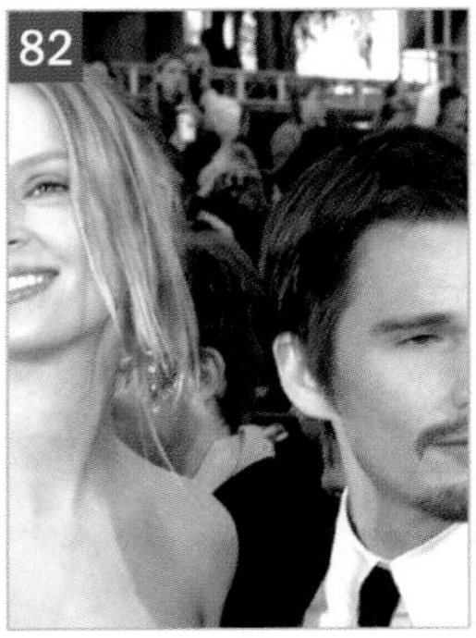


SPLITS

# Milestones

IN 2003, RUSSELL CROWE SHED HIS BOISTEROUS BACHELOR WAYS AND THE FIRST OF THE GUY *FRIENDS,* MATT LEBLANC, GOT HITCHED. SUDDENLY SINGLE GALS INCLUDED HALLE BERRY AND (MOST NOISILY) LIZA MINNELLI. MEANWHILE, BROOKE SHIELDS FINALLY BECAME A MAMA, AND SIR PAUL'S LADY, HEATHER MILLS, JOYOUSLY WELCOMED THEIR FIRST CHILD

(MAY 19TH)

# Matt LeBlanc & Melissa McKnight

After being engaged for five years, the lovable *Friends* lunk, 36, and McKnight, 38, a model, tied the knot at night at a dramatic cliff-top estate on Kauai. The attendants were McKnight's children from an earlier marriage—Tyler, 13, and Jacquelyn, 9—with whom LeBlanc had become tight. ("He's amazing with the kids," said a friend. "He's like a big kid himself, so they have a great time together.") After the ceremony, the 75 guests (including castmates Jennifer Aniston, Courteney Cox and Lisa Kudrow) pelted the newlyweds with flower petals. Everyone oohed over the Samoan fire dancers and partook of the four-tiered cake with *lilikoi* (passion fruit) filling. The couple then honeymooned on—hey, where else, man?—Kauai. Within months, the pair revealed that LeBlanc's apprentice parenthood would have a payoff. They are expecting in March 2004.

(AUGUST 23RD)

# Bart Freundlich & Julianne Moore

It was a stay-at-home wedding, but the bride, 43, donned a lilac Prada gown and earrings borrowed from friend and fellow actress Ellen Barkin. The 33-year-old groom sported a cravat. The parents of Caleb, 6, and Liv, 1, who met when Freundlich directed Moore in 1997's *The Myth of Fingerprints,* exchanged vows in a nondenominational ceremony in their backyard in Manhattan's Greenwich Village. Afterward their 32 guests (including Barkin and her husband, Revlon CEO Ron Perlman, and actor Billy Crudup) feasted on filet mignon, tuna carpaccio and four different wedding cakes. Commented one of the two chefs: "It really was a family affair."

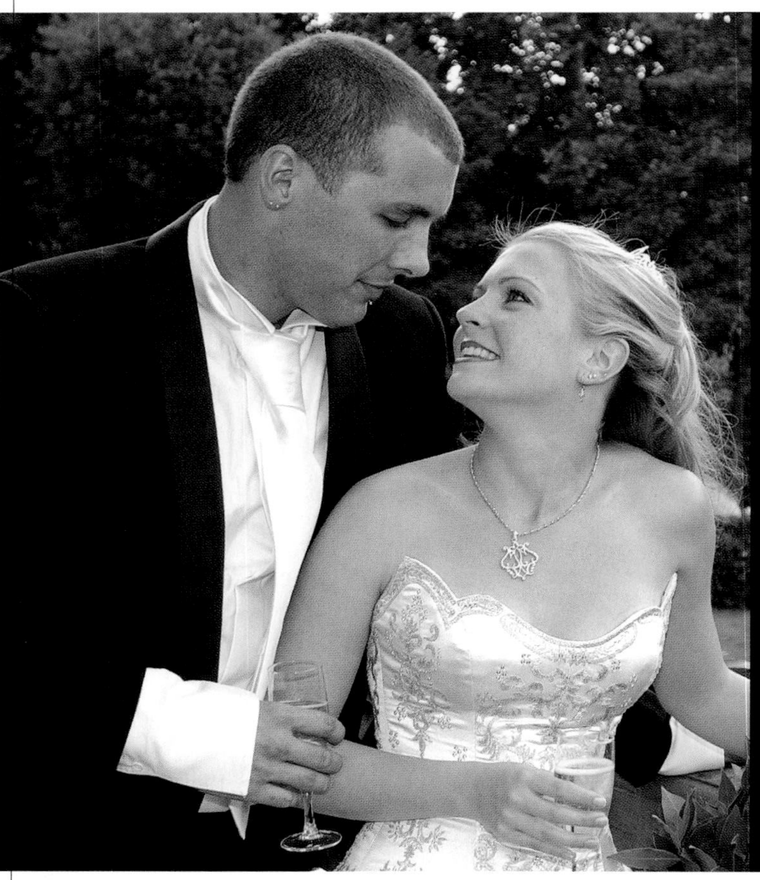

(JULY 19TH)

# Mark Wilkerson & Melissa Joan Hart

"I always wanted to get married in Italy," said Hart, 27, who shot a *Sabrina the Teenage Witch* special in Rome in 1998. Her union with Wilkerson, 26, lead singer and guitarist for the hard-rock trio Course of Nature, was celebrated at Florence's Grand Hotel Villa Cora. Among the 90 guests were *Sabrina* costar Soleil Moon Frye and the camera crew of an ABC Family reality series that chronicled the behind-the-scenes hoopla. The outdoor reception was held in 100-degree heat, and the bride later cooled her heels—literally—in the hotel fountain. Then she partied till 2 a.m. "I have to go," she explained, "or Mark is going to kill me."

(APRIL 7TH)

# Russell Crowe & Danielle Spencer

As a single bloke, Crowe had been notorious for his barroom-brawling style of life. Now here he was, nearly bawling at the altar during his wedding vows to fellow Aussie and old flame Spencer, 33, an actress-singer he had first met on the set of 1990's *The Crossing.* "He started choking up," said pal John McGrath, "then he shook his head, took a deep breath and started again." In fact, Crowe, like the indomitable sea captain he plays in *Master and Commander,* had just about everything else under control. He had planned every detail of the four-day fete at his cattle ranch in Nana Glen, Australia, beginning with the date (his 39th birthday), the location (a chapel he had designed himself for his brother Terry's 2002 nuptials) and the time of the ceremony (sunset). Bride and groom were even fashion-label coordinated. Giorgio Armani dressed him in a three-quarter-length coat and adorned Spencer in an ivory silk organza gown detailed with French Chantilly lace. At the reception, some 100 guests (including his *Gladiator* director Ridley Scott) were serenaded by Crowe accompanied by his own band, 30 Odd Foot of Grunts. All in all, a mighty g'day, mate!

(MAY 24TH)

# Judith Nathan & Rudy Giuliani

She had been the Other Woman during the then-New York City mayor's tumultuous marriage to second wife Donna Hanover. But now the previously wed Nathan, 49, was finally first lady—at least in the eyes of Giuliani, 59, as the couple tied the knot at his former official residence, Gracie Mansion. Proof of Giuliani's adoration could be seen in the Piaget pearl-and-diamond necklace he presented her right before they exchanged vows. "They're just mad for each other. That's what came through during the entire wedding," said Vera Wang, who designed Nathan's antique-white gown. Nathan also show-cased a $75,000 tiara on loan from jeweler Fred Leighton—ultimate proof she was queen for a day.

(MARCH 25TH)

## Royston Langdon & Liv Tyler

Her parents, Aerosmith frontman Steven Tyler and singer Bebe Buell, had seemingly nonstop schedules, so after months of postponements, Tyler, 26, who plays *Lord of the Rings'* ethereal elf Arwen, and Spacehog lead singer Langdon, 31, finally went ahead without them at a candlelit ceremony in a private beach house on Barbados. The groom's family did make it. "The bride looked beautiful—stunning," reported Langdon's dad, Chester, "but that's Liv all the time."

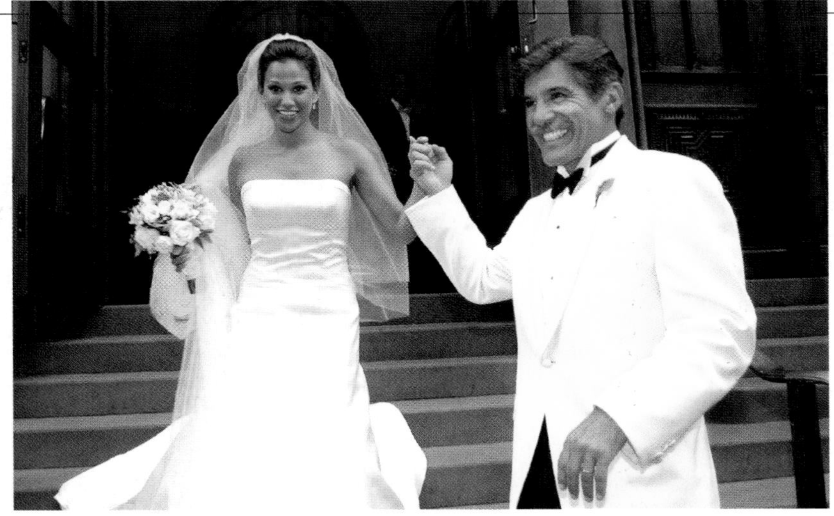

(AUGUST 10TH)

## Erica Levy & Geraldo Rivera

"I will cherish you for all time," Rivera, 60, pledged to his 28-year-old bride. "And I promise to have a good time doing it." Who could doubt his vow after watching the TV news showboat groove down the aisle of Manhattan's Central Synagogue to "Oye Como Va" followed by bridesmaids (his two daughters among them) marching to ABBA? For insurance, he had an "E" for Erica etched on his arm. "Diamonds are forever," said the five-time groom, "but tattoos are real commitment."

(MAY 10TH)

## Joshua Gruss & Shoshanna Lonstein

Lonstein, 28—who began dating Jerry Seinfeld during his show's heyday in the '90s, when she was still in her teens—has clearly grown up and moved on. The UCLA grad, now a successful Manhattan dress and swimwear designer and TV fashion commentator, tied the knot with Gruss, 29, an investment analyst for his family's New York firm. The Jewish ceremony at the city's swank Metropolitan Club featured an 18-ft.-high chuppah (the bride and groom's canopy). At 7 p.m. all eyes were on Lonstein as she walked down the aisle in a Reem Acra champagne gown and 30-carat diamond necklace. "She was laughing and crying," said one guest, "which really sums her up."

(AUGUST 9TH)

## Barrett Williams & Joey McIntyre

They met cute. Williams, 25, an L.A. real estate agent, had no idea her very first client, McIntyre, 31, was *that* McIntyre, the former New Kids on the Block singer turned actor, when she began his requested search for a rental apartment in 2002. They clicked, and . . . fast-forward one year to New York's Plaza Hotel, where Williams, resplendent in a Carolina Herrera strapless ivory silk gown, and McIntyre, in Gucci tux, were wed by a rabbi and a priest. Fellow former New Kids Jordan and Jonathan Knight joined some 230 guests. "They both looked so incredibly gorgeous," said *Sex and the City*'s Mario Cantone, a McIntyre pal. "I was so teary-eyed."

(SEPTEMBER 20TH)

## Tammy Lynn Michaels & Melissa Etheridge

The bride (Etheridge, 42) wore a beaded linen jacket and crepe trousers. The *other* bride (Michaels, 28, a TV actress) chose a matching white lace coat and gown. Both went barefoot. Okay, so it wasn't exactly a traditional wedding (gay marriages aren't recognized in California) but a commitment ceremony presided over by the Reverend Charles Hall. The couple looked "relaxed, happy, down-to-earth," said a friend, as they exchanged sunset vows—and platinum-and-diamond bands—at Dick Clark's Malibu estate. The 150 guests included Tom Hanks, Steven Spielberg and Sheryl Crow. Etheridge's two children with ex-lover Julie Cypher (via sperm donor David Crosby) also graced the joyous occasion.

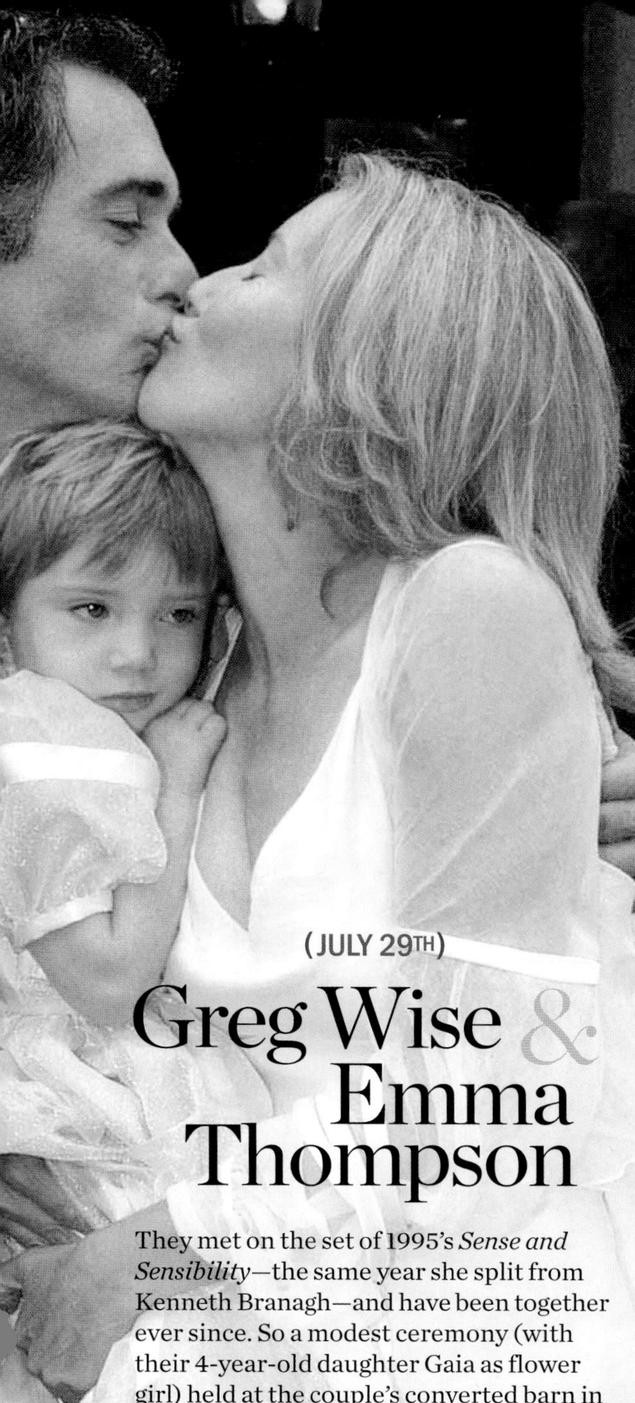

(JULY 29TH)

## Greg Wise & Emma Thompson

They met on the set of 1995's *Sense and Sensibility*—the same year she split from Kenneth Branagh—and have been together ever since. So a modest ceremony (with their 4-year-old daughter Gaia as flower girl) held at the couple's converted barn in Scotland made perfect sense for Thompson, 44, and fellow actor Wise, 37. The bride's simple Maria Grachvogel gown was a sensible choice, too. The groom's kilt? Ah, perhaps a wee unwise. Along with local well-wishers waiting to greet the couple outside the Coylet Inn, the reception site, was a swarm of insects that had come for a bite. And what more open target than the bare-legged Wise? "His manhood has been murdered," quipped Thompson. "We are bitten to death but couldn't be happier." Or, perhaps, bawdier. The couple's wedding cake resembled, "how can I put this," wondered the inn's manager, "a pair of boobs."

(JANUARY 11TH)

## Toni Collette & David Galafassi

A decade ago she played a bride in *Muriel's Wedding*. Now Collette, 31, really was one, marrying Galafassi, 25, a drummer in the Australian band Gelbison, on her 25-acre ranch. Among the 73 guests: *Muriel* costar Griffiths (see below), who declared the couple "very much meant to be."

(DECEMBER 31ST, 2002)

## Rachel Griffiths & Andrew Taylor

What more romantic way to greet 2003 than as newlyweds? Griffiths (*Six Feet Under*), 35, and her fellow Aussie Taylor, an artist who turned 35 at midnight, were united by Griffiths's uncle, a Jesuit priest, at her old Catholic elementary school in Melbourne, not far from where the couple first kissed 17 years before.

(JUNE 22ND)

# Jackie Titone & Adam Sandler

The star of *The Wedding Singer,* 37, played his zany self in front of actress-model Titone, 29, his girlfriend of six years, and 400 invitees at Dick Clark's oceanfront Malibu estate. Titone sported a Carolina Herrera gown and handmade diamond jewelry by Neil Lane. She was preceded down the aisle by the groom's pet bulldog Meatball, in tux and yarmulke, bearing the bride's wedding band on his back. "The ring was huge!" said Dylan Sprouse, 11, Sandler's *Big Daddy* costar. "I could have gone blind if I stared at it any longer." All in all, "it was a real classy affair," adjudged guest Rodney Dangerfield. "Only two fights broke out, and I made $12 parking cars!"

### (JUNE 28TH)

# Justine Maurer & John Leguizamo

She's Jewish, he's Catholic, so the wedding of Maurer, 35, an estate planner, and actor-comedian Leguizamo, 43, with whom she's lived for six years, was, in a word, eclectic. Son Lucas, 2, was the ring bearer and daughter Allegra Sky, 3, the flower girl. The 30 friends and relatives invited to the couple's upstate New York lakefront home danced to "Hava Nagila" as well as to salsa and hip-hop. At the ceremony itself, the groom, famed for his one-man shows (*Freak, Sexaholix . . . A Love Story*), suddenly got "very choked up," he said, after seeing his bride enter in a Calvin Klein gown with her own diamond tiara. "It was," he said, "like seeing a vision."

### (OCTOBER 11TH)

# Alyson Hannigan & Alexis Denisof

Oh, the agonies Hannigan, 29, and Denisof, 37, faced back when they were engaged and costarring (as Willow and Wesley, respectively) on *Angel*, the *Buffy the Vampire Slayer* spinoff. Recalled Denisof: "I kept looking at her, and inside I kept giggling and I kept thinking to myself, 'I have to remember I'm in a scene. I can't just smile at my fiancée.' But really all I wanted to do was run over and give her a hug." All that repressed ardor was finally released during a wedding blast at Palm Springs' Two Bunch Palms Resort & Spa. The guests enjoyed all the house amenities for three days, and the ceremony itself was "very soulful," said event planner Rob Smith. "Everyone felt they were part of something really beautiful." Still, the newlyweds may soon find their *Angel*ic togetherness coming to an end: NBC is developing a sitcom for Hannigan to headline.

(JULY 5TH)

## Heather McComb & James Van Der Beek

"It was magical—the sun was setting when they said their vows," reported the wedding planner for *Dawson's Creek* star Van Der Beek and actress McComb, both 26. It was also ambrosial. The couple were hitched at Saddlerock Ranch in Malibu under an aromatic arch of jasmine, honeysuckle and pale-lilac roses.

(OCTOBER 12TH)

## Elisa Atti & Evan Handler

The bride's Italian relatives needed an interpreter. Still, there was no mistaking the mood at the Manhattan-restaurant nuptials of Atti, 33, a medical researcher, and *Sex and the City*'s Handler, 42. Observed the manager of the eatery: "She was giggling and just looked so happy," and the ceremony, which took place on an overhead balcony, "was very *Evita*esque."

(JULY 11TH)

## Jamie-Lynn Sigler & A.J. Discala

Nothing could put a damper on the Brooklyn Botanic Garden nuptials of Sigler, 22 (Tony Soprano's daughter Meadow), and Discala, 32, her manager and beau of two years. Certainly not the torrential downpour that erupted just as the ceremony began. And not even the 10 minutes it took to free Sigler's older brother Adam (entrusted with the wedding rings) from a locked bathroom. Well, there was one moist moment: When Sigler saw her groom waiting for her at the end of the aisle, she began to sob. "I was overcome with joy," she said.

(JULY 19TH)

# Leah Remini & Angelo Pagan

Remini, 33, who plays acerbic housewife Carrie Heffernan on CBS's *The King of Queens,* has been known to bicker on the set with her TV spouse, Kevin James. It sounds not unlike Remini's edgy rapport with Pagan, 45. "We can tell each other anything," said the actor and salsa musician. "Even if it hurts sometimes." But other times it tickles. When the bride (who wore a Les Habitudes ivory gown) and groom exchanged their own vows at the Four Seasons in Las Vegas, "the words were very funny, very heartfelt," noted *King* producer Rob Schiller, one of the 125 guests at the poolside ceremony. Remini thanked Pagan for "giving her some soul" through salsa lessons; he thanked her for making him a better dad to his three sons from previous relationships. Said Schiller: "It brought tears to everyone's eyes."

# Births

(OCTOBER 28TH)

## Paul McCartney & Heather Mills

It's a girl! Despite one British tabloid's erroneous report that Sir Paul, 61, and second wife Mills, 35, had a new male heir to be called Joseph, the bemused parents quickly set the record straight. "She is a little beauty," they declared of Beatrice Milly. "We are ecstatic." Just as they were the year before, when Mills—who had feared she would be unable to conceive because of two ectopic pregnancies she'd suffered during her first marriage—discovered that she was pregnant with Beatrice. "We both started crying, and it was just a miracle," the ex-model turned anti-land-mine activist told Larry King. Both she and McCartney (who has three children and a stepdaughter by his late first wife, Linda) were stunned anew when the lass arrived, at a London hospital, three weeks early.

(MAY 15TH)

# Brooke Shields & Chris Henchy

I'm amazed every day, watching Brooke and the baby," said Henchy, 39. "It's amazing to see a living soul that has come from this marriage." Shields, 38, shared her husband's incredulity over the long-awaited arrival of Rowan Francis, who weighed in at 7 lbs. 5 oz. After their April 2001 wedding, the couple met with frustration and heartache trying to conceive. Shields already knew that scar tissue on her cervix (resulting from treatment of abnormal cells) made parenthood an iffy proposition. Then, in early 2002, three months after starting in vitro fertilization, she suffered a miscarriage. "We were crushed," she said. Yet undeterred. After attempting six more IVFs over the next eight months, the Henchys finally got news in August 2002: Shields was pregnant with Rowan. Their daughter's birth, however, did not come easily. After 24 hours in labor, Shields underwent a C-section. Nowadays their good-natured infant commutes between homes in Manhattan and L.A. with her dad (executive producer of *I'm with Her,* an ABC sitcom based on their lives) and mom, who's eyeing her own sitcom—and other projects closer to home. "I'd rather Rowan not be an only child," Shields said. "I really want to have other children."

(MARCH 1ST)

## Jessica & Jerry Seinfeld

Talk about a stand-up dad. Just a few months before the birth of Julian Kal, his second child with wife Jessica, 32, Seinfeld, 49, was already kvetching to a Manhattan comedy-club crowd about the joys of raising their first, 3-year-old Sascha. "Why," he asked, "would you want something in your life that stands in the middle of your living room, looks you in the eye and then poops in their pants?" Good question. Undoubtedly, as soon as he learns to talk, Julian will have a snappy reply.

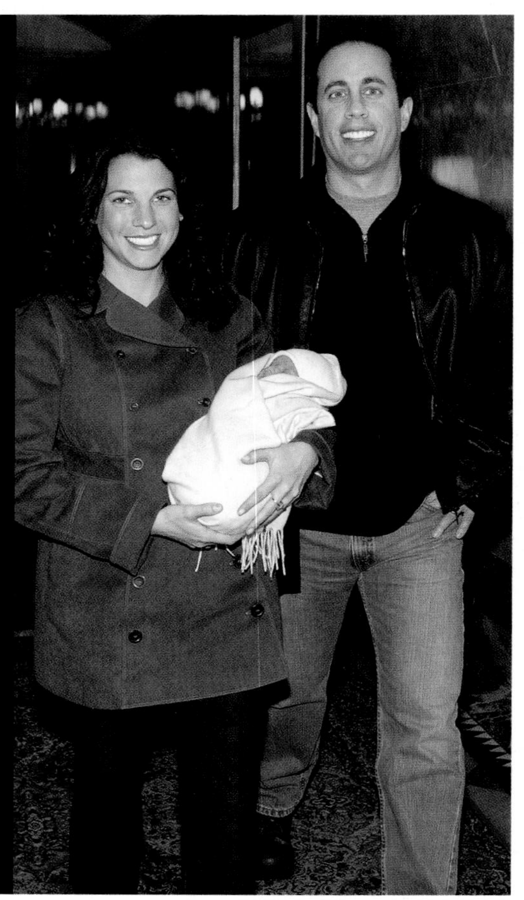

(JUNE 28TH)

## Tim Montgomery & Marion Jones

His parents are the world's fastest man and woman, which may explain why Timothy "Monty" Montgomery got off to a very fast start—arriving three weeks before the due date of Jones, 28, an Olympic gold medalist. Boyfriend Montgomery, also 28, who holds the record in the 100-meter dash, was competing at a track meet in Scotland when he got news of Monty's arrival and rushed home to meet his son in a Raleigh, North Carolina, maternity ward. So is he destined to follow in his parents' track shoes? Not according to Mom, who said, "I told Monty, 'You have no pressure on you. You enjoy your life.'"

(JANUARY 30TH)

## Matthew Vaughn & Claudia Schiffer

"Meeting Matthew and having Caspar have been two of the most important moments of my life," said the German supermodel, 33, of her spouse, 32, and their first child. Schiffer and British film producer Vaughn (*Lock, Stock and Two Smoking Barrels*) met at an L.A. dinner party in 2001 and wed a year later. He was at her side when she delivered their son by C-section at a London hospital. "Caspar," said his mom, "is beautiful and amazing, and I couldn't be happier." Or luckier. Three months later, Schiffer, Vaughn and Caspar all escaped injury when their Range Rover collided with a van in London.

(JUNE 10TH)

## Joan Lunden & Jeff Konigsberg

Lunden, 53, the former *Good Morning America* cohost, tried in vitro fertilization at first. But after five attempts, she and Konigsberg, 42, a summer-camp owner, turned to surrogate mother Deborah Bolig. The happy result: twins Max Aaron and Kate Elizabeth.

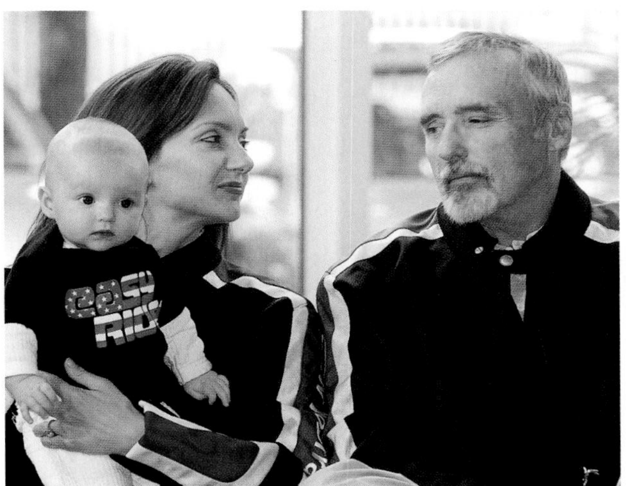

(MARCH 26TH)

## Victoria Duffy & Dennis Hopper

"I'm not proud of a lot of [my] work . . . but I need to keep working all the time," Hopper, 67, has said. "I've been married five times and I have children to support." The latest offspring of the prolific actor-director (*Easy Rider, Blue Velvet*) is Galen Grier, his fourth, and first by Victoria, 35, his actress wife of seven years.

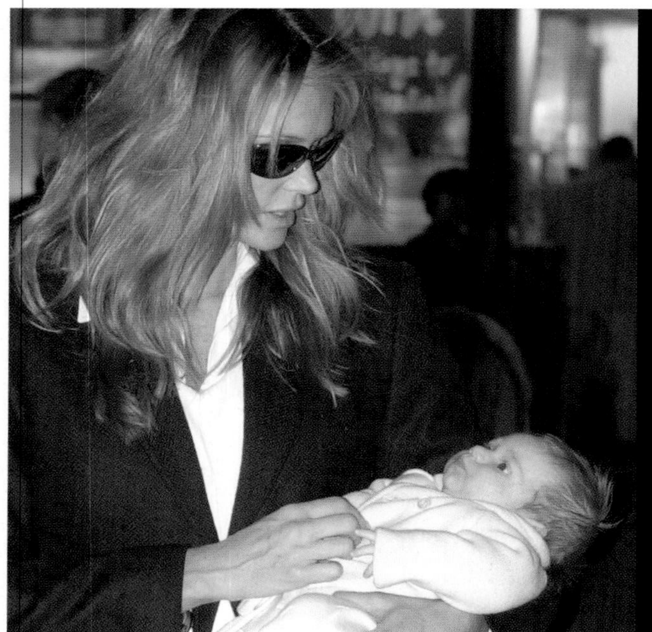

(FEBRUARY 4TH)

## Elle Macpherson & Arpad "Arki" Busson

"The birth of my sons. The birth of new emotions. What a blessing!" exulted supermodel Macpherson, 39, a few months after son Aurelius Cy had joined her, his brother Arpad Flynn, 5, and their dad, Busson, 40, Elle's French financier boyfriend, in the family's posh digs in London's Notting Hill. In September, however, Macpherson reportedly entered an Arizona rehab program for postpartum depression and exhaustion. Several weeks later she emerged, saying she felt "fabulous."

(JANUARY 13TH)

## Luciano Pavarotti & Nicoletta Mantovani

It's safe to say few proud papas can sing lullabies as forcefully as Pavarotti, 68. When Alice, his daughter by longtime girlfriend Mantovani, 34, was wailing her heart out one day, "I vocalized for her with a full tenor for the first time," he said. "I was ferocious. She stopped, and I said, 'Thank you very much.'" In fact, Pavarotti has other reasons to be thankful for Alice: Her fraternal twin, Riccardo (who would have been the singer's first son), was stillborn. The Modena, Italy-based opera great, who has three adult daughters by his ex, "was mourning nonstop," said a friend. "But Alice was like a ray of sunshine in a dark room." Born premature and weighing just 3 lbs., she required three weeks in an incubator before she could breathe on her own. Her dad kept a nightly vigil. "She really wanted to live," said Mantovani (who by year's end became Mrs. Pavarotti), "and she had strong lungs from her father." As for Dad's pipes, in October he released his first solo studio album in more than 15 years. The title song, "Ti Adoro (I Adore You)," is dedicated to Alice.

(FEBRUARY 24TH)

# Kelly Ripa & Mark Consuelos

Ripa, 32, had some great news for her *Live with Regis and Kelly* cohost: the birth, minutes earlier, of son Joaquin. Unfortunately "they wouldn't let me make a call from the OR," she told Philbin—and millions of TV fans—by phone the next day. Ripa and Consuelos, 31, her husband and former costar on *All My Children,* already had another son, Michael Joseph, 5, and a daughter, Lola Grace, 2. On *20/20,* Ripa hinted to Barbara Walters that their brood might expand further. "I'm a big fan," she said, "of even numbers." Though now juggling two shows—*Live* and her new ABC sitcom *Hope & Faith*—Ripa revealed that in 10 years "I see myself as a full-time mom." When informed that Kelly and Mark had yet to pick a middle name for their newborn, Philbin coyly suggested, "Name him Joaquin R, but don't let people know what the *R* is; just you and I know." When Ripa returned to *Live* from maternity leave in April, she brought along 2-month-old Joaquin Antonio, the middle name honoring her father-in-law. Sorry, Reege. Better luck with No. 4.

(NOVEMBER 3RD)

# David Letterman & Regina Lasko

It was a rare peek through the *Late Show* funnyman's famously curmudgeonly facade. "I could never imagine ever being a part of something that turned out this beautiful," Letterman, 56, told his audience the night after girlfriend Lasko, 43, gave birth to their first child, Harry Joseph (named after Letterman's father), in a New York City hospital. But Dave, being Dave, couldn't resist the wisecracks, even compiling his own Top 10 list of Reasons I'm Excited to Be a Father. (No. 2: Two words: Swedish nanny.) Then, with a mad glint, Harry's dad confided, "First thing, I took him home and dangled him over the balcony."

# Splits

(16 MONTHS)

## David Gest & Liza Minnelli

The wacko wedding (with Elizabeth Taylor and Michael Jackson as attendants) was an ominous start. But with concert producer Gest, 50, pulling the strings, Minnelli, 57, at first lost 90 lbs., booked a tour and addressed her alcoholism, and the pair constantly expressed gooey affection. "Every night I go home and fill my baby with love," bragged Minnelli of her fourth hubby. Then came the clamorous aborting of their VH1 reality show, and after their July separation, Lorna Luft claimed that he had turned her half sister into "a freak show." Gest countered with a $10 million civil suit charging that she beat him so severely during vodka-fueled rages that he suffers from vertigo, hypertension and phonophobia (morbid fear of sounds, including one's own voice). Minnelli, who filed divorce papers the next day, pleaded for "mutual respect and dignity." Gest's allegations, she said, were "hurtful and without merit."

(5 YEARS)

## Sharon Stone & Phil Bronstein

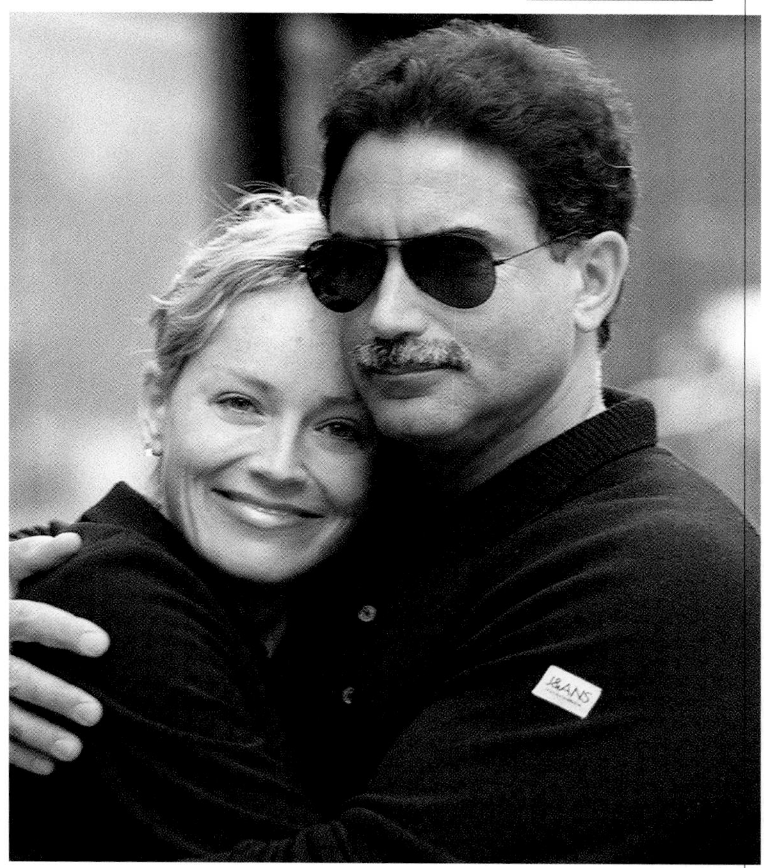

Ray Charles performed at their 1998 wedding, but the tune slowly changed from "It Had to Be You" to "Hit the Road, Jack." Twice-married Stone, 45, and thrice-wed *San Francisco Chronicle* editor Bronstein, 53, had been social fixtures in the City by the Bay. She stood by him during his '99 angioplasty and his '01 severed tendon after being chomped by a Komodo dragon in a freak accident at the L.A. zoo. He was at her bedside as she recuperated from a life-threatening brain hemorrhage later that year. But Bronstein, described by a crony as "a workhorse," was often in the newsroom, and his wife on location or filming in L.A. "They just drifted apart," said a friend. "There is not a third party involved." The divorce filed by Bronstein suggests that he may challenge the prenup, which reportedly grants him $1 million. He also filed for joint custody of their son Roan, 3. "They will attempt," said his lawyer Nordin Blacker, "to work it out."

(4½ YEARS)

## Kim Cattrall & Mark Levinson

"Mark taught me about patience and understanding," *Sex and the City*'s Cattrall once said of audio-equipment mogul Levinson, 57. The pair even collaborated on a how-to manual, *Satisfaction: The Art of the Female Orgasm*. But shortly after its '03 publication, the satisfaction was over. A rep maintained that the two are just "taking a break." The thrice-married Cattrall, 47, reported that she was trying to adjust to dating again. One problem: Her public persona means that her escorts wind up on the gossip pages. While she laughs off the scrutiny, she feels for those sharing her limelight. "My gay friends are photographed with me, and then people think they're heterosexual," noted Cattrall. "It's not very good for them."

(9 YEARS)

## Ricki Lake & Rob Sussman

In 1994, Sussman, an illustrator, fretted that he was marrying above his credit-card limit. Having talk host wife Lake support him seemed, he said, "emasculating." Apparently. The pair sought couples therapy just months after their Las Vegas wedding, and in '03 the TV star, 35, gave Sussman, 37, his walking papers not long after they moved into a $6.5 million L.A. mansion. Lake, according to insiders, is seeking custody of their sons Milo, 6, and Owen, 2.

(2 YEARS)

## Brandy & Robert Smith

"It was kind of fun," said the singer and sitcom star, 24, of her hasty, top-secret wedding to music producer Smith, 23, in the summer of '01. Even the bride's mother wasn't told. Not so much fun was their parting of ways in July, which seemed equally abrupt and mysterious. "They remain friends," said a Brandy rep, "and will continue to jointly raise their daughter," Sy'rai, 1. Her pal Karu F. Daniels said the couple's relationship had been strained for some months. Still, he added, "I do believe she loved him."

(2½ YEARS)

## Scott Foley & Jennifer Garner

After meeting Foley on the set of *Felicity* in 1998, Garner recalled that their two-year courtship grew "gradually." The same could not be said of the *Alias* star's skyrocketing career, which was targeted as a possible reason for their split. Speculation circulated that Foley, 31, was jealous of his wife's higher profile. Though she conceded that issue may have been "in there somewhere," TV's sexy superspy, also 31, turned coy when pressed further: "I don't know—ask me in a year."

(5 YEARS)

## Lance & Kristin Armstrong

Some five weeks after winning his fifth Tour de France trophy, the cyclist reached the finish line of his marriage. The couple, both 32, grew apart as he led his worldwide quest and she stayed home in Austin, Texas, with son Luke, 4, and twins Isabelle and Grace, 2. Wrote Lance in his memoir: "All I knew was that in trying to do everything, we'd forgotten to be married."

(13 YEARS)

## Kerry Kennedy & Andrew Cuomo

Kennedy's camp announced that the Democratic duo's June separation was "amicable." Hardly. Shortly after, the former U.S. Housing Secretary, 46, issued a statement accusing RFK's daughter, 44, of adultery. No stranger to scandal, Kerry's Uncle Ted said, "She's a wonderful mother [to three daughters], and we're behind her 100 percent."

(5 YEARS)

# Ethan Hawke & Uma Thurman

An admired bohemian couple went bust when tabloids revealed Hawke's indiscretions with Jennifer Perzow, 22, whom he met on location in Montreal. (She works at a family clothing firm.) Upon his return home to Manhattan, Hawke, 33, checked into a hotel. Thurman, also 33, put on a brave face and continued to promote *Kill Bill Vol. 1.* "It's very difficult, but the pros of having a family have been amazing for me," said Thurman of kids Maya Ray, 5, and Levon Roan, 2. "I am just trying to figure things out." But Uma's little brother Mipam had apparently already resolved the situation for himself. "I want to kill him," he told New York's *Daily News.* "I can't believe what he's done to my sister."

(4 YEARS)

## Juliette Lewis & Steve Berra

Actress Juliette met her Romeo, a pro skateboarder, through little sister Brandy Lewis, one of only six guests who attended their 9/9/99 mountainside ceremony in Big Sur, California. An ingenue always on fast forward, she became Brad Pitt's girlfriend at 16, raked in an Oscar nod at 17 and then entered drug rehab at 23. A couple of years later, Lewis swapped vows with Berra after only a few months of dating. "They're best friends who made each other laugh," said Brandy of the couple, both 30. But the giggles ceased in April, when Lewis trotted out the divorce documents.

(3 YEARS)

## Salma Hayek & Edward Norton

A closemouthed couple ended their liaison as they began it—quietly. One minute Norton, 34, was escorting longtime girlfriend Hayek, 37, to the Oscars (where she and her pet project *Frida* were up for six Oscars, including Best Actress). The next, each had seemingly moved on. The actor-writer-director was spotted in New York City squiring an unknown blonde. Across the country, the actress-producer linked herself to a more recognizable, and rugged, golden-haired boy: *Sweet Home Alabama* star Josh Lucas, 32.

(4 YEARS)

## Raquel Welch & Richard Palmer

"Marriage isn't easy," said Welch, 63, just before her fourth trip up the aisle. "But this time I'm in it for the whole ride." Alas, in '03 the journey was halted with a joint announcement of their separation. Palmer, 49, co-owns an L.A.-based restaurant chain with his former girlfriend, actress Cathy Moriarty.

(9 YEARS)

## Michael Sheen & Kate Beckinsale

No reason was given for the end of the long, unwed relationship of *Pearl Harbor* star Beckinsale, 30, and actor Sheen (*The Four Feathers*), 34. But six months later, the actress, who had daughter Lily, 4, with Sheen, was engaged to Len Wiseman, who directed her in the 2003 vampire flick *Underworld*.

(3 YEARS)

## Halle Berry & Eric Benét

After finding himself in the tabloids for a fling with an ex-girlfriend in '02, R&B singer Benét confessed to the embarrassed Berry, also 37, that he "had made terrible mistakes" and checked into rehab for sex addiction. Berry stood by him at first, citing her commitment to India, 11, his daughter from a previous relationship. "I'm all she's got as far as a mother goes," said Berry. (India's mother was killed in a car accident in '93.) But in the fall, the Oscar winner sparked rumors after passionately kissing Limp Bizkit frontman Fred Durst in a music video for the *Gothika* soundtrack. "Eric and I have had marital problems for some time now and are trying to work things out," she told the press. "However, at this point, I feel we need some time apart to reevaluate our union."

(15 YEARS)

## Danny Mozes & Cynthia Nixon

On *Sex and the City*, her super-cynical character had just settled in with her Mr. Right. So it was a sad irony that Nixon, 37, split from photographer Danny Mozes, also 37, after a 15-year relationship. The former college sweethearts and parents to Samantha, 7, and Charles, 1, separated over the summer, conceding that they were "growing apart." But, assured her rep, "there were no third parties involved."

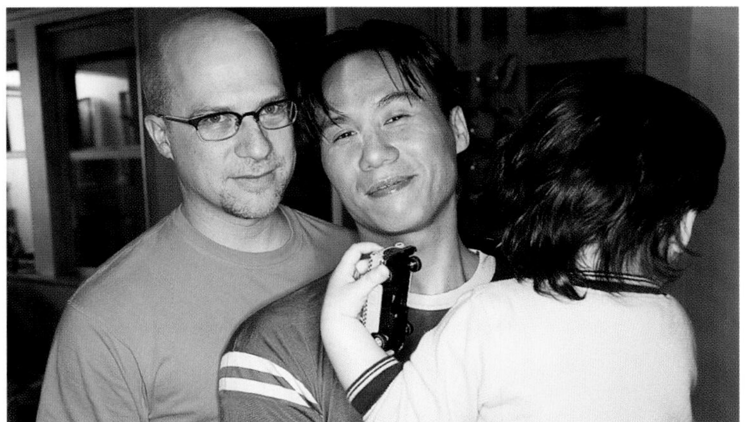

(15 YEARS)

## Richie Jackson & B.D. Wong

Although Wong (center), 43, who plays Dr. George Huang on NBC's *Law & Order: Special Victims Unit,* and partner Jackson, 38, decided to separate, they continued to share custody of their 3-year-old son Jackson Foo Wong, who was born to a surrogate. The boy is the subject of Wong's book *Following Foo,* which chronicles the child's struggle for life after being born 11 weeks premature.

## HOLLYWOOD'S

# Big nights

TINSELTOWN TINGLED WITH THE UNEXPECTED TRIUMPH OF FIRST-TIMERS LIKE NORAH JONES AND ADRIEN BRODY. BUT IN OUR MEMORY BANKS, THE OSCARS' BEST ACTOR WINNER AND THE GLITTERING AWARDS SHOWS OF 2003 WILL BE FOREVER SEALED WITH ...

# ...a kiss

GRASPING HALLE BERRY, BRODY DELIVERED THE SMOOCH THAT UNLEASHED A THOUSAND LIPS

ohosts **GARRY SHANDLING & BRAD ARRETT** opened the Emmys spoofing MTV's epic exchange (see right).

**BRITNEY SPEARS & MADONNA** kicked off the Video Music Awards, not to mention all blonde inhibitions.

**MATTHEW PERRY** gave Emmy winner **DORIS ROBERTS** another high. "Wow, that was worth coming up here for," she sighed.

# the Oscars

## 75TH ANNUAL ACADEMY AWARDS

PRESENTED MARCH 23, 2003

**BEST PICTURE**
*Chicago*

**BEST DIRECTOR**
Roman Polanski, *The Pianist*

**BEST ACTRESS**
Nicole Kidman, *The Hours*

**BEST ACTOR**
Adrien Brody, *The Pianist*

**BEST SUPPORTING ACTRESS**
Catherine Zeta-Jones, *Chicago*

**BEST SUPPORTING ACTOR**
Chris Cooper, *Adaptation*

**BEST ORIGINAL SCREENPLAY**
Pedro Almodóvar, *Talk to Her*

**BEST ADAPTED SCREENPLAY**
Ronald Harwood, *The Pianist*

**BEST FOREIGN LANGUAGE FILM**
*Nowhere in Africa*

**BEST SCORE**
Elliot Goldenthal, *Frida*

**BEST SONG**
Eminem, "Lose Yourself," *8 Mile*

**Halle Berry**
The show went on four days after the war began in Iraq, so the dress code was relatively subdued. Berry opted against glittery jewelry and asked designer Elie Saab to add tulle to her gown's bare places.

**Nicole Kidman**
Kidman (in Jean Paul Gaultier couture) shared her finest hour with daughter Isabella, 10, who was on the money when she whispered to Mom right before her Oscar was announced, "You're going to win."

## Queen Latifah

An ice princess by design, Best Supporting Actress nominee Queen Latifah jazzed up her Halston with a $2.9 million diamond-studded clutch and 12-carat earrings.

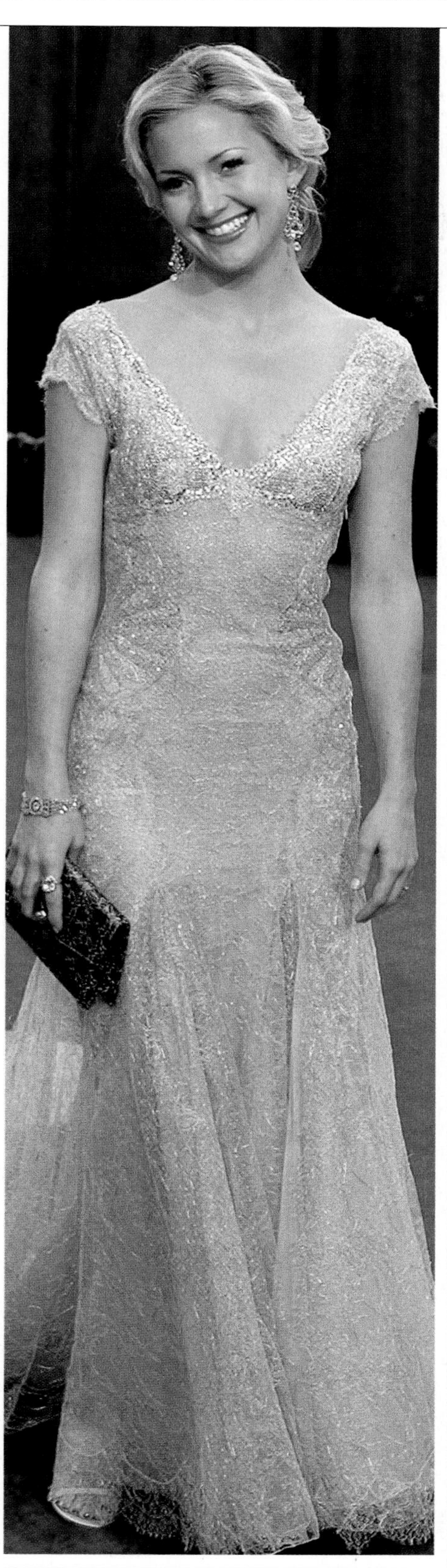

## Kate Hudson

Hudson set a new gold standard in fashion, donning an Atelier Versace gown stitched with threads of the precious metal. Hours spent laboring over the handmade lace? 300. Her Oscar entrance? Priceless.

## Catherine Zeta-Jones

"My hormones are way too out of control to be dealing with this!" joked the *Chicago* star (in a couture chiffon Versace). She was eight months pregnant when she accepted her Best Supporting Actress honor.

## Gwen Stefani

The lead singer of No Doubt flaunted camouflage and fishnets onstage. But off, Stefani sought "more glamor" and slipped into a Vivienne Westwood reminiscent of old Hollywood.

## Norah Jones

Showcasing Oregon designer Michelle DeCourcy, Jones upset Bruce Springsteen for Album of the Year—one of five awards she juggled home. Her other high of the evening? "Meeting Aretha Franklin, Bonnie Raitt and Cyndi Lauper."

# the Grammys

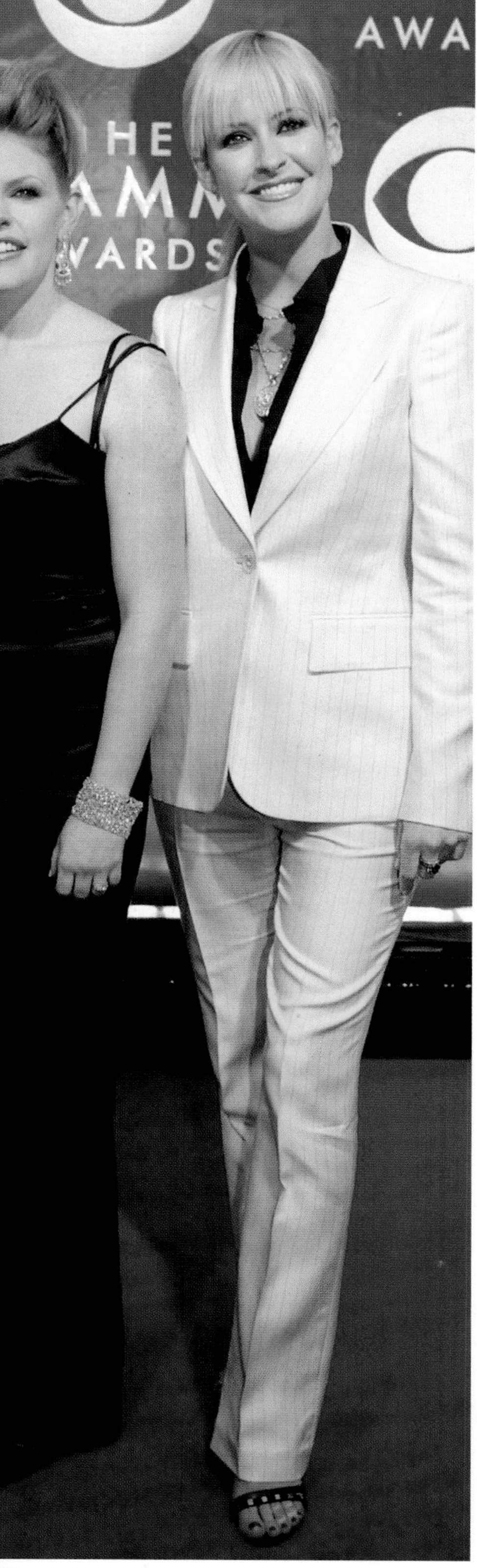

**Dixie Chicks**
Natalie Maines—flanked by Emily Robison and Martie Maguire—thanked her steel-guitarist dad, Lloyd Maines, for coproducing their album *Home.* The trio also collected awards for best vocal and instrumental performances.

**Ashanti**
In Roberto Cavalli at her maiden Grammy appearance, the Princess of Hip-Hop and Soul celebrated with a victory for her self-titled CD in the contemporary R&B category.

## 45TH ANNUAL GRAMMY AWARDS

PRESENTED FEBRUARY 23, 2003

**RECORD OF THE YEAR**
*Don't Know Why,*
Norah Jones

**ALBUM OF THE YEAR**
*Come Away with Me,*
Norah Jones

**SONG OF THE YEAR**
"Don't Know Why,"
Jesse Harris

**POP VOCAL, FEMALE**
"Don't Know Why,"
Norah Jones

**POP VOCAL, MALE**
"Your Body Is a Wonderland,"
John Mayer

**POP VOCAL, GROUP**
"Hey Baby," No Doubt

**R&B ALBUM**
*Voyage to India,* India.Arie

**COUNTRY ALBUM**
*Home,* Dixie Chicks

**RAP ALBUM**
*The Eminem Show,* Eminem

**ROCK ALBUM**
*The Rising,*
Bruce Springsteen

**POP VOCAL ALBUM**
*Come Away with Me,*
Norah Jones

**BEST NEW ARTIST**
Norah Jones

# the Emmys

55TH ANNUAL EMMY AWARDS

PRESENTED SEPTEMBER 21, 2003

**DRAMA SERIES**
*The West Wing*

**COMEDY SERIES**
*Everybody Loves Raymond*

**ACTRESS, DRAMA**
Edie Falco, *The Sopranos*

**ACTOR, DRAMA**
James Gandolfini, *The Sopranos*

**ACTRESS, COMEDY**
Debra Messing, *Will & Grace*

**ACTOR, COMEDY**
Tony Shalhoub, *Monk*

**SUPPORTING ACTRESS, DRAMA**
Tyne Daly, *Judging Amy*

**SUPPORTING ACTOR, DRAMA**
Joe Pantoliano, *The Sopranos*

**SUPPORTING ACTRESS, COMEDY**
Doris Roberts, *Everybody Loves Raymond*

**SUPPORTING ACTOR, COMEDY**
Brad Garrett, *Everybody Loves Raymond*

**MINISERIES**
*Steven Spielberg Presents "Taken"*

**MADE-FOR-TV MOVIE**
*Door to Door*

**Ray Romano**
TV's highest-paid actor wore Hugo Boss to present Bill Cosby with the Bob Hope Humanitarian Award before joining the *Everybody Loves Raymond* cast to receive its first Outstanding Comedy Series honor.

**Sarah Jessica Parker**
Like a kid in a couture candy store, the *Sex and the City* star gushed over her confection from Chanel. "It reminded me of cotton candy," Parker said. "I can't believe I got to wear it."

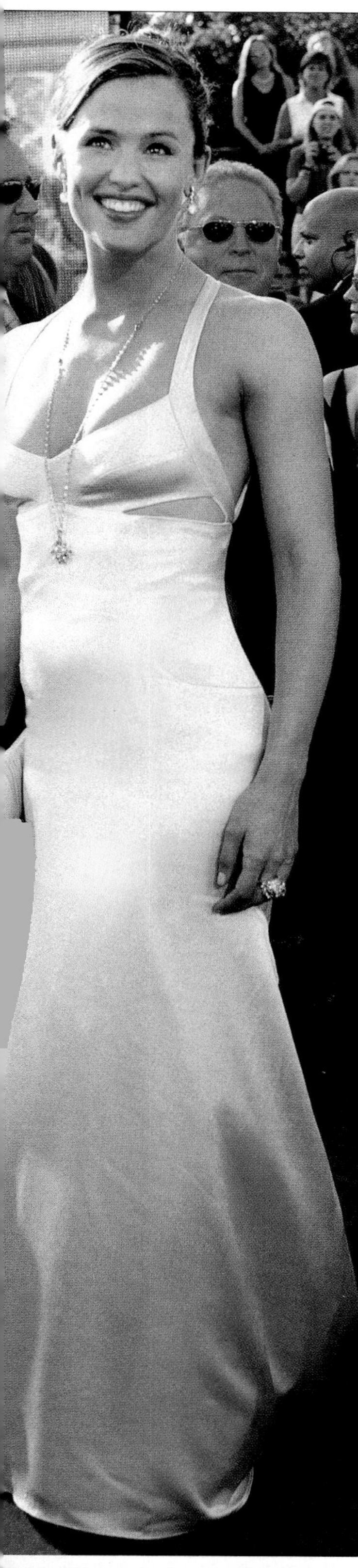

## Jennifer Garner

Garner added glitz to a Narciso Rodriguez gown with Neil Lane diamonds. But her dates were down-to-earth: her folks instead of boyfriend Michael Vartan, her *Alias* costar.

## Michael Chiklis

The *Shield* lead lost the Emmy to James Gandolfini, and then he lost his Hugo Boss pants. Chiklis donated them to Clothes Off Our Backs, a celebrity auction that raises money for autism research.

## Debra Messing

At last! A four-time nominee for *Will & Grace,* she giggled and yelped when she accepted her prize. "This is otherworldly," said Messing, whose Elie Saab gown made her feel "like a modern Rita Hayworth."

# the MTV Awards

## 12TH ANNUAL MTV MOVIE AWARDS

PRESENTED MAY 31, 2003

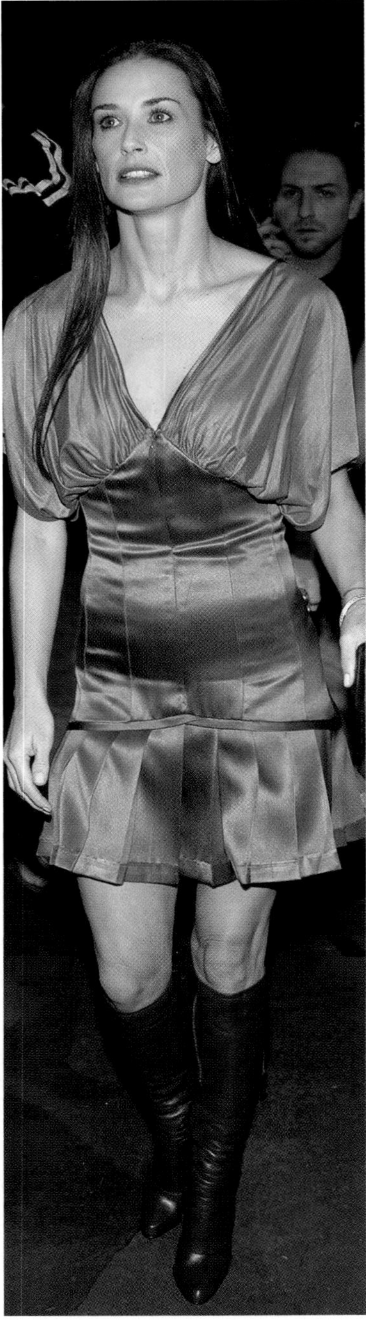

### Demi Moore

Greeted by raucous applause, the *Charlie's Angels* villain (in Catherine Malandrino) presented the Best Male Performance award to Eminem.

### Beyoncé

Bound in Versace, Beyoncé added some bling from sister Solange. The necklace "is my good luck," said the Breakthrough Female Performance nominee for *Austin Powers in Goldmember.* In the end, Jennifer Garner triumphed for *Daredevil.*

### P. Diddy & Ashton Kutcher

Evoking images of the Rat Pack, Diddy helped his copresenter adopt a Sinatra look. Kutcher's usual T-shirt and trucker hat gave way to Tom Ford.

## Justin Timberlake

A kid at heart, the soloist (who came sans girlfriend Cameron Diaz) topped off his sharp suit with sneakers and hailed one of his three awards as "cooler than bubble gum."

## Christina Aguilera

The "Dirrty" diva preened in pink feathers by Roberto Cavalli. But *Queer Eye for the Straight Guy*'s fashion guru Carson Kressley nixed her dress, snipping, "She looked like a Vegas showgirl."

## 50 Cent

The Best New Artist in a Video defined dapper in a pin-striped Versace suit. He later trumped mentor Eminem to nab his second moonman of the evening for Best Rap Video.

**Jennifer Aniston**
Baring herself in a jersey dress by Giorgio Armani, the *Friends* nominee lost for the second straight year to Megan Mullally of *Will & Grace.*

**Uma Thurman**
Aglow in a sherbet-colored Chanel, the willowy actress attended the SAG stag. At the time she was still with husband Ethan Hawke, who stayed home to babysit their two kids.

## 9TH ANNUAL SCREEN ACTORS GUILD AWARDS
PRESENTED MARCH 9, 2003

## 60TH ANNUAL GOLDE[N] GLOBE AWARDS

**Renée Zellweger**
A showstopper in vintage Valentino, Zellweger was named Best Actress for the musical *Chicago.* Richard Gere was also victorious for his tap-dancing role in the movie.

PRESENTED JANUARY 19, 2003

## Kim Cattrall

"You have no idea how many men I've had to sleep with to get this award," quipped *Sex and the City*'s Valentino-clad seductress. She bested Cynthia Nixon for a Supporting Actress Globe.

## Keith Urban

The Australian native sang "Raining on Sunday" at the Las Vegas ceremony but lost out in the best single category to Kenny Chesney, who also won Top Male Vocalist.

## Shania Twain

Emerging from a 2½-year sabbatical, the pop-country princess received a nomination for Top Female Vocalist only to be one-upped by repeat winner Martina McBride.

## 38TH ANNUAL ACADEMY OF COUNTRY MUSIC AWARDS

PRESENTED MAY 21, 2003

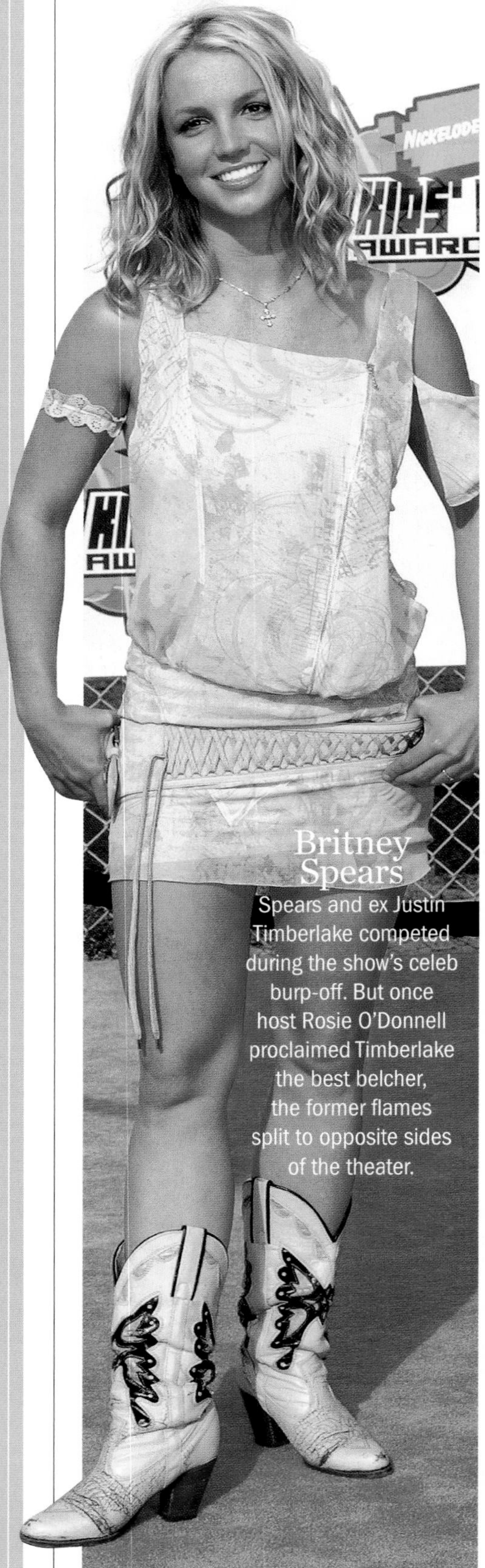


## Britney Spears

Spears and ex Justin Timberlake competed during the show's celeb burp-off. But once host Rosie O'Donnell proclaimed Timberlake the best belcher, the former flames split to opposite sides of the theater.

## Kelly Osbourne

Her album *Shut Up* didn't go platinum, but who's to say her locks can't? Fresh off her first tour, the newly blonde bombshell grilled celebs on the orange carpet for a post-awards special.

# 16TH ANNUAL KIDS' CHOICE AWARDS

PRESENTED APRIL 12, 2003

# 5TH ANNUAL TEEN CHOICE AWARDS

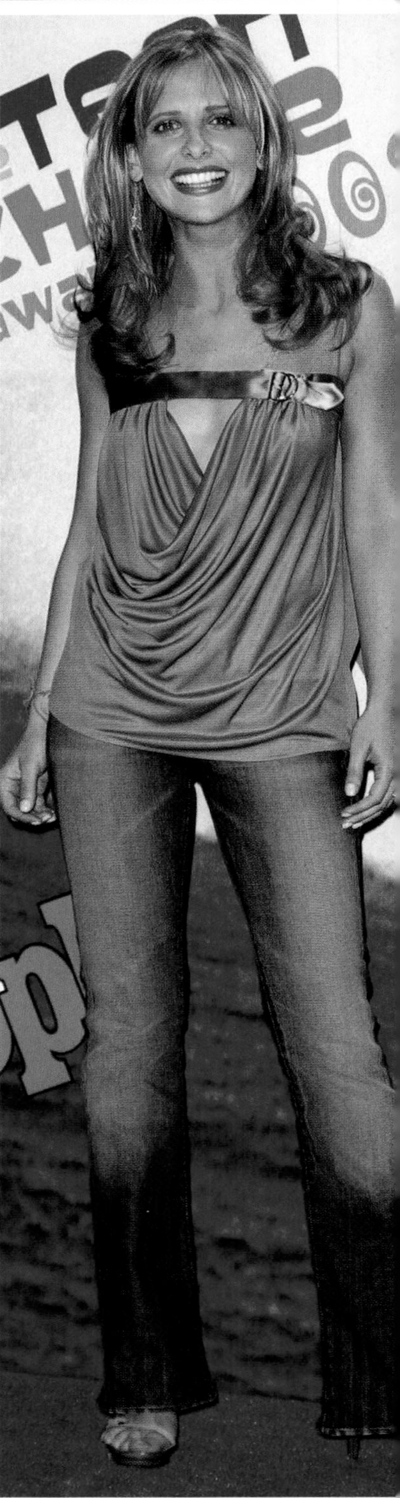

## Sarah Michelle Gellar

*"Buffy,* in this incarnation, is over," declared Gellar, defecting to focus on her movie career. Heartbroken if loyal, teens anointed the ex-vampire slayer Choice TV Actress of '03.

PRESENTED AUGUST 6, 2003

## Hilary Duff

Though she lost the Choice Female Hottie title to Beyoncé, the Queen of Tweens collected the Choice Breakout Movie Star surfboard for adapting *Lizzie McGuire* to the big screen.

## Faith Hill

Just back from a Bahamas getaway, the country crooner swapped flip-flops for Louis Vuitton heels to accept her third People's Choice prize. Now, said Hill, she has "one for each daughter."

## Matthew Perry

It came full circle for Perry, who accepted favorite-sitcom laurels for *Friends.* "Nine years ago we won best new show," he said. "And here we are winning best show—well, that's kind of neat."

29TH ANNUAL PEOPLE'S CHOICE AWARDS

PRESENTED JANUARY 12, 2003

# Katharine Hepburn

## A DAZZLING TRAILBLAZER CHANGED OUR IDEA OF WHO WORE THE PANTS

Wickedly smart and irascibly outspoken onscreen and off, Connecticut Yankee Katharine Hepburn collected a record four Best Actress Oscars and transformed the image of a Hollywood leading lady. In an era when studios dictated how their employees must dress, the star of *The Philadelphia Story* and *On Golden Pond* took her own cues, donned man-tailored trousers and became a fashion icon. Her fierce independence, though, was tinged with a thoroughly human weakness. Once divorced, she maintained a 27-year love affair with the alcoholic and married Spencer Tracy. Proudly nonconformist, Hepburn lived life on her own terms. "If you obey all the rules," she once said, "you miss all the fun."

# 2003 Tributes

WE BID A BITTERSWEET FAREWELL TO THE LUMINARIES WHO LEFT US IN 2003. WE THANK BOB HOPE FOR THE MEMORIES AND MISS THE WEEKLY COMPANY OF JOHN RITTER. WE HEAR IN OUR HEARTS THE MUSIC OF JOHNNY CASH, BARRY WHITE AND CELIA CRUZ. THE GRACE OF THOSE GREAT GREGORYS—PECK AND HINES—SURVIVES ON DVD. AND WE STILL TREASURE HIM IN RERUNS, BUT THE NEIGHBORHOOD WILL NOT QUITE BE THE SAME WITHOUT FRED ROGERS

# John Ritter

**A BELOVED PERFORMER WHO DELIGHTED TWO GENERATIONS OF SITCOM FANS, HE LIVED BY SIMPLE—AND GENEROUS—RULES**

With a gift for the goofy, a sweet tooth for slapstick and boundless energy, John Ritter warmed his castmates' and his fans' lives for three decades. On the racy *Three's Company* he played randy bachelor Jack Tripper, living with two babes (Suzanne Somers and Joyce DeWitt). Ritter, whose father, Tex Ritter, was a singing cowboy on radio and screen, originally assumed *Company* would be "a one-joke show—and then we'd be looking for work again." But it ruled for seven seasons, establishing Ritter as a household name. He went on to headline shows like *Hooperman,* a detective series, stretched to play a sad sack in *Sling Blade* on the big screen, and enlivened character parts from a minister on *The Waltons* to a legal client on *Ally McBeal.* Twice married (to actresses Nancy Morgan and Amy Yasbeck), Ritter was a devoted father of five, who rearranged his schedule to be part of their lives. He struck gold again in '02 as the put-upon dad of *8 Simple Rules for Dating My Teenage Daughter.* But his great heart finally gave out in September. Falling suddenly ill on the set, he died of a ruptured cardiac artery mere hours later. It was his daughter Stella's 5th birthday and just six days before his own 55th. "We lost a good one," says Somers. "His hat was full of tricks, and I think he still had a few left."

1916-2003

# Gregory Peck

## THE MOVIES' GRAND OLD MAN STOOD FOR THE DECENCY IN US ALL

Nine days after his indelible Oscar-winning character, lawyer Atticus Finch in *To Kill a Mockingbird,* was voted by the American Film Institute as the top hero in movie history, Gregory Peck died at 87 of what was described as old age. With him went an age as well, one when a screen hero could conquer with compassion instead of karate. "He understood the doubts and disappointments of the decent man," said director Martin Scorsese, who cast the actor in his 1991 remake of *Cape Fear* (Peck had starred in the 1962 original). His charisma in more than 50 films—they included comedies like *Roman Holiday,* thrillers like *Spellbound* and epics like *Moby Dick*—reached out to all demographics. Women responded to his thinking man's magnetism; men admired his stoic self-confidence. The only child of a La Jolla, California, pharmacist father, Peck was himself the dad of five, and his second marriage, to Veronique Passani, a French newspaperwoman, lasted 48 years. The star devoted much of his offscreen time to promoting nuclear disarmament and gun control, and to stumping for liberal politicians. Indeed, Peck was successful enough to make Richard Nixon's "enemies list." "He cared deeply about people and justice," said Mary Badham, who played his daughter in *Mockingbird.* "And he loved to laugh."

# Gregory Hines

## WITH HIS AMAZING GRACE, HE PUT TAP BACK ON ITS FEET

He scares me to death," Sammy Davis Jr. once said of Gregory Hines, "because his potential is as big as a mountain." It was a mountain that the New York City-raised actor and musical star moved with his feet. Like Davis, Hines was a child performer, dancing professionally with his brother Maurice Jr. (father Maurice played drums) from the age of 6. Later he almost single-handedly revived the art of tap. To do so, Hines said, "you have to be aggressive, inventive and resilient." So he was. He won Tony nominations for his exuberant moves in musicals including *Eubie!* and *Sophisticated Ladies* and took home the Best Actor prize for 1992's *Jelly's Last Jam*. Onscreen he danced through *The Cotton Club* and matched steps with Mikhail Baryshnikov in *White Nights*. More recently he had a recurring role on TV's *Will & Grace*, playing Grace's bedroom-eyed beau. Hines faced personal problems that included cocaine use and two divorces. But, said son Zach, one of the star's three children, "nobody could have hoped to have a better father." Diagnosed with liver cancer a year before his death, Hines kept his condition mostly to himself. His greatest gift, said Camryn Manheim, who briefly dated Hines in 1998, "was making the people around him happy."

1911-2003

# Hume Cronyn

### A CHAMELEON IN GREASEPAINT, HE WAS ONE OF AMERICA'S GREATEST CHARACTER ACTORS

A casting director once told Hume Cronyn, "You may have a difficult time, because you don't look like anything." But the gods of showbiz turned the elfin, untypable Canadian into a much sought-after man for all parts. He earned raves on Broadway in works like *The Gin Game* and *A Delicate Balance* and won his first Tony in '64 as Polonius in Richard Burton's *Hamlet.* He became more widely known in his 70s for his roles in film comedies, including *Cocoon* and its sequel. In those movies, and often onstage, Cronyn paired with his wife, Jessica Tandy, the *Driving Miss Daisy* Oscar winner. Married for 52 years, they were the theater's first couple, honored with Lifetime Achievement Tonys shortly before her death in '94. (Cronyn later married children's author Susan Cooper.) His formula for inhabiting such a range of characters was simple. "If you're doing the devil, look for the angel in him," he explained. "If you're doing the angel, look for the devil in him."

1924-2003

# Celia Cruz

### A DAZZLING DIVA ADDED A DASH OF *'AZUCAR!'* TO SALSA

Only two months after a brain tumor was removed, an ebullient Celia Cruz laid down tracks for a new album, adding to her 70-some career releases. It didn't take a brain surgeon to discover the dauntless spirit of the Havana-born diva. During her waning months before succumbing to cancer, the boisterous salsa singer—known to punctuate her songs with the joyous cry *Azúcar!* ("sugar")—still donned her trademark Cruz couture: a flamboyant gown topped with a vibrant wig and soaring high heels. In 1997, samples of that signature costuming were enshrined in the Smithsonian.

Defecting from Castro's Cuba in 1960, Cruz vowed never to return "until it is free." She was touring Mexico at the time, and with her was Pedro Knight, her trumpeter and, later, music director and (since 1962) beloved husband. Branded a traitor, Cruz was denied reentry, even for her mother's funeral. "I keep thinking about Cuba," she said. "It always hurts me." But the U.S. and the world welcomed her fusion of Latin and international beats. She went on to collaborate with the likes of Tito Puente, Luciano Pavarotti and Gloria Estefan and won five Grammys (three of them Latin). "She left more than No. 1 hits," said producer Emilio Estefan. "She left a legacy of love."

1932-2003

# Johnny Cash

## THE MAN IN BLACK BROUGHT LIGHT AND 'FIRE' TO THREE GENERATIONS OF LISTENERS

"This is a travesty!" rocker Justin Timberlake told the audience at the 2003 MTV Video Music Awards, after winning Best Male Video. "My grandfather raised me on Johnny Cash, and I think he deserves this more than any of us." If the Man in Black had scored for his video "Hurt," it would have added to an extraordinary vault. The Arkansas sharecropper's son collected 11 Grammys for his 1,500 songs and 100 original albums. His anthems of love and loss included "Cry, Cry, Cry," "I Walk the Line" and "Folsom Prison Blues," all delivered in a quavering baritone as deep as a hand-dug well. Cash's personal life played like a country tune. "Ring of Fire," a 1963 tale of forbidden love sung with tour partner June Carter, foreshadowed the doom of his marriage to Vivian Liberto. Cash and Carter got divorces, then wed each other in 1968; she became his helpmate also in battling his amphetamine addiction. "Our hearts are attuned to each other," he said. "I can't imagine living without her." She died in May, and, plagued by asthma, glaucoma and a depleted immune system, Cash worsened, dying of respiratory problems connected to diabetes four months later. His funeral near their Hendersonville, Tennessee, home was attended by a who's who of American music, from Willie Nelson to Kid Rock. Ray Charles sent a simple note with his flowers: "I can't stop loving you." Who could?

1929-2003

# June Carter Cash

## COUNTRY'S QUEEN HELPED HER HUSBAND WALK THE LINE

June Carter had a unique split-rail alto and impeccable lineage. She was one of three performing daughters of the legendary Mother Maybelle Carter, who helped transform country music from pickin' to singin' in the '20s. Managed by Col. Tom Parker, June played gigs with another of his acts, Elvis. She went on to earn three Grammys and act in series like *Gunsmoke* and films like Robert Duvall's *The Apostle.* Upon first meeting Johnny Cash backstage at the Grand Ole Opry in '56, she could not look him in the eye because, she recalled, "I would be drawn into his soul and I never would have been able to walk away." When he became her third husband, they melded a family of his four daughters (including singer Rosanne) and her two. They later had a son together. Said Merle Kilgore, her "Ring of Fire" coauthor, after her death following heart surgery: "She was everybody's rock."

1948-2003

# Lynne Thigpen

**A FORMER TEACHER LENT HER CELLO-LIKE VOICE TO AWARD-WINNING FILMS, THEATER AND TV SHOWS**

"My grandmother used to say, 'Fry the bacon while the pan is hot,' so I do as much as I can." Did she ever. Known for her deep voice, Lynne Thigpen was a much-in-demand actress who bagged a Tony for *An American Daughter* and had roles in films from *Tootsie* to *Anger Management.* She played the Chief in PBS's long-running *Where in the World Is Carmen Sandiego?* and costarred on *The District.* Her longtime companion, computer programmer Larry Aronson, was by her side at her death of a cerebral hemorrhage. Thigpen was, said pal Morgan Freeman, "just one of those people whose work you know and admire."

1915-2003

# Andrew Heiskell

**A CREATIVE PUBLISHER, HE BECAME A CIVIC LEADER**

Andrew Heiskell came to the U.S. from Europe at 20, later joined the editorial staff of LIFE, and at 30 became its publisher. In 1973, as Time Inc. chairman, it was his idea to launch PEOPLE. He devoted his retirement to many causes, including the rescue of the New York Public Library.

1933-2003

# Nina Simone

**THE 'HIGH PRIESTESS OF SOUL,' SHE SANG OUT ON CIVIL RIGHTS**

Nina Simone's 1991 autobiography is titled *I Put a Spell on You* for good reason. It was the title of one of her songs, and it's how she affected devotees for three decades. The Juilliard-trained pianist-vocalist combined jazz, blues and folk with her own smoky intensity. Her only Top 20 hit was 1959's "I Loves You, Porgy," but Simone, who lived in France and died of natural causes, cut more than 40 albums and wrote the bitter and unforgettable civil rights anthem "Mississippi Goddam" after the killing of four black children in Birmingham, Alabama, in 1963. "Nina Simone was a messenger," said bassist friend Me'Shell NdegéOcello, "to our heart and conscience."

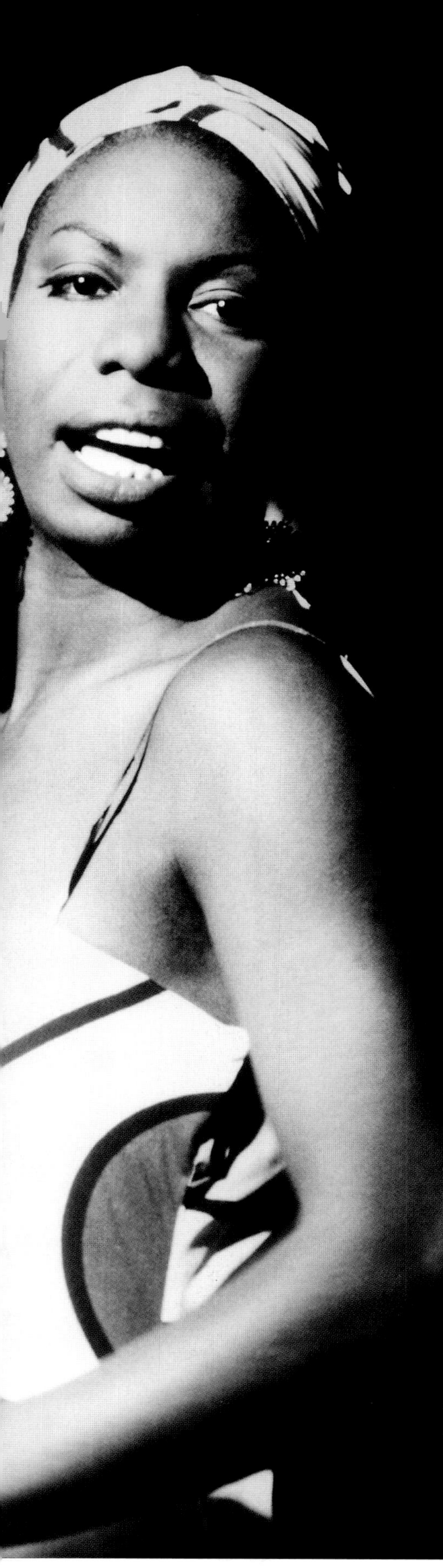

1909-2003

# Elia Kazan

## THE MOST DAZZLING ACTORS' DIRECTOR BECAME, TO SOME, A PUZZLING TURNCOAT

"I coulda been somebody, instead of a bum," says Marlon Brando's battered ex-pug in *On the Waterfront.* The director of that movie classic, Elia Kazan, was thought variously to have been both. He had helped refine Brando's craft on Broadway with *A Streetcar Named Desire* and won three Tonys. His 19 films, including *A Face in the Crowd* and *East of Eden,* racked up 21 Oscars. "He pointed the way to a new kind of moviemaking," said Martin Scorsese, "brutally honest and emotionally overwhelming." Emigrating from Turkey at 4, Kazan attended Yale Drama School and briefly joined the Communist Party. When he turned over names of other members during the 1950s Red hunt, some friends felt betrayed. But in 1998 he received a Lifetime Achievement Oscar. Said his third wife, Frances: "I don't think Elia had any regrets."

1928-2003

# Fred Rogers

D THREE GENERATIONS, HE WAS AMERICA'S FAVORITE NEIGHBOR

It was always a beautiful day in the neighborhood when soft-spoken Fred Rogers, a Presbyterian minister from Pittsburgh, put on his cardigan and transported millions of kids to a make-believe place where he could speak frankly about the most real of issues—anger, loneliness, war, disability. Children's worst fears, he believed, had to be "manageable and mentionable." Never patronizing or preachy, *Mister Rogers' Neighborhood* made the young feel good about themselves. A vegetarian and dedicated swimmer, Rogers, who had two sons of his own, was a magnetic figure even without his sweater. "I was privileged to meet him twice at the White House," recalled First Lady Laura Bush, "and he was even more gentle and reassuring in person."

1924-2003

# Leon Uris

HIS EPICS BROUGHT HISTORY TO LIFE

Leon Uris's chunky "nonfiction novels," including *Exodus,* about Israel's founding, sold 150 million copies worldwide, turning a high school dropout into a brand-name author. Thrice married, the Marine vet also scripted film adaptations for his own works, like *Battle Cry* and *Topaz.* Literary critics carped that his characters were wooden and plots creaky, but countered fellow writer Pete Hamill: "None of that matters, as you are swept along in the narrative."

1965-2003

# Trevor Goddard

A YOUNG ACTOR'S DEATH SHOOK UP HOLLYWOOD

Trevor Goddard, whose credits included *Pirates of the Caribbean* and TV's *JAG,* was divorcing Ruthann, his wife and mother of their two sons, when he died of a possibly accidental drug overdose. The English-born actor, who long suffered from old boxing injuries, had been put on new painkillers after hurting his leg during the *Pirates of the Caribbean* shoot.

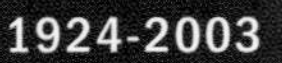
1924-2003

# Buddy Hackett

## HIS RUBBER FACE MEANT RAUCOUS LAUGHTER IN CLUBS AND IN MOVIES

"A priest, a porcupine and a prostitute go into a bar. The priest says to the porcupine, 'Pretend she's with you.'" That was the announcement on Buddy Hackett's answering machine at the time of his death. The rotund, baby-faced comic tested his craft as a teen in New York's Catskills while his upholsterer father repaired furniture. "I can make people laugh at will," he decided. "It was a gift from God." He graduated in 1954 to Broadway, starring in *Lunatics and Lovers.* The exposure led to TV, headlining the 1956-57 sitcom *Stanley,* which helped launch Carol Burnett; and in 1958-59 he replaced Art Carney on *The Jackie Gleason Show.* His movies included *It's a Mad, Mad, Mad, Mad World* and *The Love Bug.* Hackett, who is survived by his wife, Sherry, a former mambo teacher, and three children, took heat for being far less PG in clubs. "Compared to motion pictures," he retorted in 1996, "I'm very mild."

1919-2003

# Robert Stack

## E DEFINITIVE G-MAN WAS A STRAIGHT SHOOTER

Asked what he did in WWII, Robert Stack, a former Navy gunnery officer, would say, "I taught machine gun." With the same rumbling, gritty delivery, the onetime national skeet-shooting champion also blasted into TV as crusading federal agent Elliott Ness in the classic series *The Untouchables* (1959-63). Stack won an Emmy for the role, which followed a 1956 Oscar nomination for his portrayal of an alcoholic in *Written on the Wind.* Later the actor, the son of an affluent California family, couldn't escape type-casting and made a number of forgettable films and returns to series TV. Stack even spoofed his tough-guy image in comedies including *Airplane!* and *Caddyshack II.* Then, beginning in 1989, the married father of two revisited his sleuthing roots as host of *Unsolved Mysteries.* Showbiz, the six-decade veteran once said, is "like being a member of this club. And you're invited in, and you hope that your invitation holds out for good." His did.

1930-2003

# Herbie Mann

## HE BROUGHT SOMETHING FRESH TO JAZZ—HIS FLUTE

As a kid in Brooklyn, Herbie Mann played sax. But when he took up the flute, an odd instrument for bebop, he started to stretch the jazz genre. A constant explorer, he fused Brazilian, African and Japanese music into his work. His own origins were reflected in an album titled *Eastern European Roots.* Mann, who died of prostate cancer, left behind writer-actress wife Susan Arison, four children and two Top 40 hits of the '70s. "To most jazz critics," he said of his unusual mass appeal, "I was basically Kenny G."

1952-2003

# Michael Jeter

## HE WAS A CLOWN LOVED BY ALL AGES

His red mustache and playful air made Tony winner Michael Jeter a hit with kids, who knew him as the Other Mr. Noodle on *Sesame Street*. Grown-ups admired his Emmy-winning turn in *Evening Shade* (1990-94) and his film roles in *The Green Mile* and *Patch Adams*. "I often see myself in my private life as being a pinched and confined person," said Jeter. "When I get onstage, I can open up."

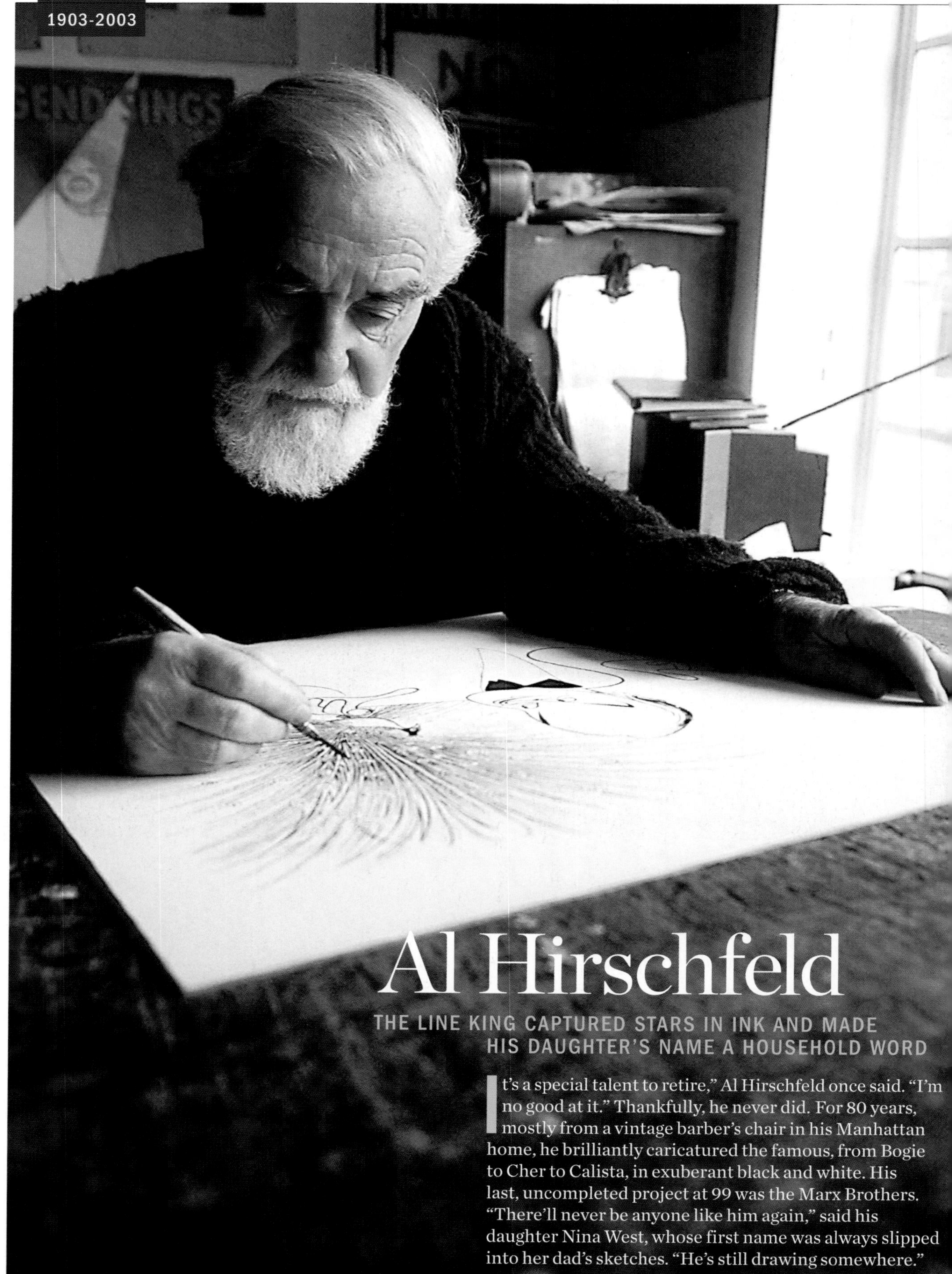

# Al Hirschfeld

## THE LINE KING CAPTURED STARS IN INK AND MADE HIS DAUGHTER'S NAME A HOUSEHOLD WORD

It's a special talent to retire," Al Hirschfeld once said. "I'm no good at it." Thankfully, he never did. For 80 years, mostly from a vintage barber's chair in his Manhattan home, he brilliantly caricatured the famous, from Bogie to Cher to Calista, in exuberant black and white. His last, uncompleted project at 99 was the Marx Brothers. "There'll never be anyone like him again," said his daughter Nina West, whose first name was always slipped into her dad's sketches. "He's still drawing somewhere."

927-2003

# Althea Gibson

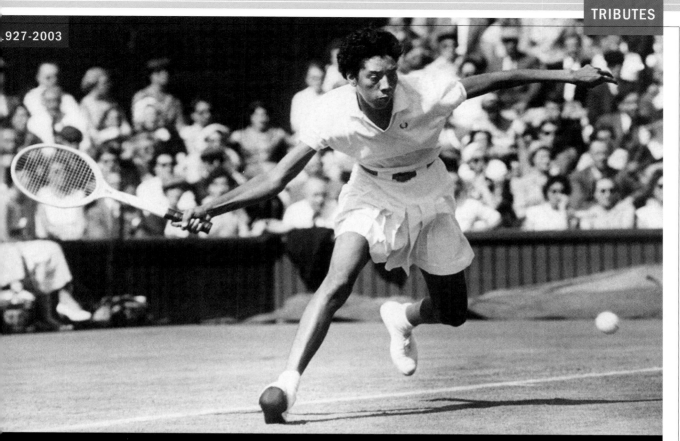

**WITH A STEELY SERVE AND IRON WILL, SHE WENT FROM HARLEM TO CENTER COURT**

Before the 2000 Wimbledon final, Venus Williams sought advice from an ideal source: Althea Gibson. In 1950 the Harlem-raised daughter of sharecroppers had broken tennis's color barrier at New York's Forest Hills, then the site of the U.S. Open. Gibson, the first African-American at Wimbledon as well (boxer Joe Louis paid for her plane ticket), won 56 tournaments. She also recorded a vocal album and in the '60s became the first black woman on the pro golf tour. In retirement she served as New Jersey's athletic commissioner. "Her road to success was a challenging one," said Billie Jean King, "but I never saw her back down."

1932-2003

# Gordon Jump

**HE ENLARGED HIS FAME AND BUILT A SECOND CAREER PLAYING AN UNDEREMPLOYED MAN**

From 1989 until shortly before his death from respiratory illness, Gordon Jump was one of TV's most recognized faces: Ol' Lonely, the Maytag repairman. The Ohio native, who was married with five children, also had character parts on *Get Smart, The Partridge Family* and *The Mary Tyler Moore Show*. Much earlier, he had worked at a string of midwestern TV and radio stations—experience that he capitalized on in the other capstone of his career: playing befuddled station owner Arthur Carlson on the hit sitcom *WKRP in Cincinnati.*

# Daniel Patrick Moynihan

1927-2003

## A DOCKWORKER TURNED SCHOLAR AND SENATOR, HE PUT SOCIAL IDEAS INTO ACTION

"If you don't have 30 years to devote to social policy," Daniel Patrick Moynihan liked to say, "don't get involved." As good as his word, he was a key adviser in the Nixon, Ford, Kennedy and Johnson administrations, became ambassador to India and the U.N. and served four terms as Democratic senator from New York. Coming of age on Manhattan's mean streets as a shoeshine boy and longshoreman, he wound up a Harvard professor and author of 18 books. Flexing his intellectual muscle on issues ranging from redressing racism to welfare reform, Moynihan was hailed by *The Almanac of American Politics* as "the nation's best thinker among politicians since Lincoln." When he died from complications of a ruptured appendix, he left his wife of 47 years, Elizabeth Brennan, and three children. "There isn't any way that anyone will fill his place in the Senate," said the woman elected to try, Hillary Clinton.

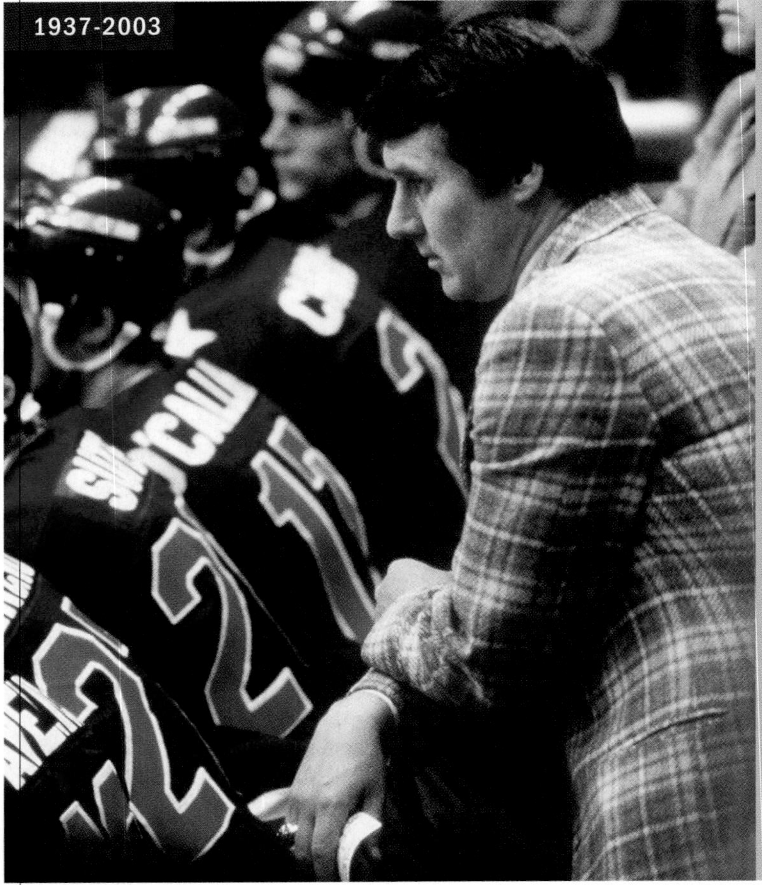

1937-2003

# Herb Brooks

## IN '80, HIS UNLIKELY YOUNG TEAM PULLED OFF THE 'MIRACLE ON ICE'

When Herb Brooks looked at an empty hockey arena, he said, "All I see are possibilities." Brooks, who died in an auto accident near his Minnesota home, also envisioned the impossible. With the authoritarian manner of an old-line coach and with fresh ideas about a faster, more open game, he inspired an unheralded bunch of college kids to pull off what SPORTS ILLUSTRATED declared the premiere athletic moment of the 20th century. At the Lake Placid Games in 1980, his underdog U.S. Olympians upset the vaunted Soviets 4-3 in the semifinal. Brooks and his Boys of Winter became instantly famous around the world for what was called the "Miracle on Ice." (It was almost an anticlimax when they beat Finland in the final for the gold.) Brooks went on to coach four NHL teams before returning to pilot Team USA to a silver medal in the 2002 Olympics. Said his '80-star-turned-NHL-scout Ken Morrow: "Coach may have been the greatest innovator the sport ever had."

# Nell Carter

## SHE DAZZLED, THOUGH LIFE GAVE HER THE BLUES

She longed to be, she said, "Judy Garland without the tragedy." Before an audience, Nell Carter indeed seemed so blessed. With a powerhouse voice that blended Bessie Smith gutbucket with Dinah Washington silkiness, the 4′11″ Alabaman was a Broadway dynamo for a decade, notching a Tony in 1978 for the Fats Waller musical *Ain't Misbehavin'*. Then in the '80s, her appealing brashness translated to TV stardom. She gained two Emmy nominations and a nationwide following as Nell Harper, mother hen to a widower's brood on the sitcom *Gimme a Break*. But adversity stalked her personal life. "It was amazing she could perform with her struggles," said *Break* costar Kari Michaelsen. Carter had been raped at 15 (daughter Tracey Hardy was born afterward). A recovering alcoholic and cocaine addict, she suffered from diabetes and underwent brain surgery for aneurysms. Carter battled her weight for decades and lost 170 lbs. in the last year of her life. Twice married and divorced, in later years she lived quietly with business partner and friend Ann Kaiser, with whom she adopted two infant sons. After her death at 54, actor friend Andre DeShields spoke for many when he said, "I'm going to miss that brass band that lived in her throat."

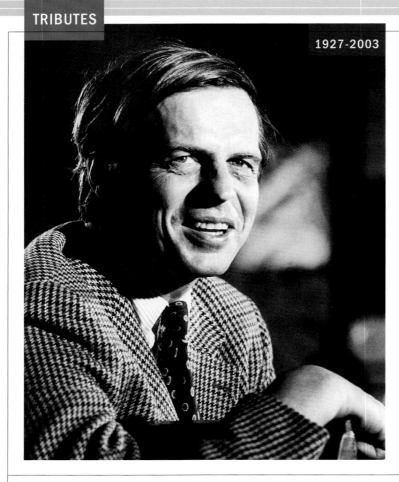

1927-2003

# George Plimpton

## A MAN OF LETTERS AND GUTS, HE WAS A HIGHLY PROFESSIONAL AMATEUR

An aficionado of pyrotechnics, George Plimpton was for years New York City's honorary commissioner of fireworks, and indeed, whatever he turned to lit up our world. An elegant and patrician ambassador's son, he wanted to try everything once. He turned four plays as a quarterback in an NFL scrimmage (he lost 34 yards) into the 1963 bestseller *Paper Lion.* He clanged the triangle with the New York Philharmonic, fought a bull and did a film cameo in *Lawrence of Arabia.* The twice-married father of four was also paterfamilias to fellow writers, founding the respected *Paris Review,* which introduced the likes of Jack Kerouac and V.S. Naipaul. Of his 2003 gig as a voice on *The Simpsons,* he beamed, "I think that means I've made it."

1949-2003

# Maurice Gibb

## HE WAS THE GLUE THAT HELD THE BEE GEES TOGETHER

Maurice Gibb was the funny Bee Gee. "He would never walk into a room," said older brother Barry. "He would prance." The Australia-reared pop trio (which also included Maurice's twin, Robin) sold over 110 million records, including the disco-defining *Saturday Night Fever* soundtrack. (A fourth Gibb, teen heartthrob Andy, died at 30 in 1988.) Maurice's drinking drowned his first union with British pop star Lulu and threatened his second to restaurant manager Yvonne Spencely, mother of their two children. Miami-based Gibb got sober in the '90s, but his death during stomach surgery made him the second brother to go before his time.

# Charles Bronson

**HE SHOWED A ROUGH-RIDER FACE TO THE WORLD BUT HAD A TENDER TOUCH AT HOME**

Director John Huston called Charles Bronson's screen persona "a grenade with the pin pulled." "I supply a presence," agreed the leathery actor, whose legacy lives in action standards like *The Dirty Dozen, The Magnificent Seven* and the cult classic *Death Wish.* Offscreen, his slow-burning squint turned to an artist's eye. One of 15 children born to Lithuanian immigrants in Pennsylvania coal country, he was a lifelong painter of some skill. And with second wife Jill Ireland, he raised a family of seven—his, hers and theirs. "He played such a tough guy," said publicist friend Lori Jonas, "yet he was such a loving father." Ireland, his costar in 11 films, died of breast cancer in 1990, plunging Bronson into despair until 1998, when he wed actress Kim Weeks. "He seemed to have come to a very peaceful time in his life," said pal Sally Kellerman after his death of pneumonia. "There was a lightness in him."

1908-2003

# Buddy Ebsen

## A HAPPY HOOFER TURNED TV HILLBILLY

Long, lean and affable, 6′3″ Buddy Ebsen was the complete entertainer. He sang and danced his way from the vaudeville stage into '30s movie musicals, including *Captain January* with Shirley Temple, who called him "a wonderful tapper and a genuinely nice guy." He would have played Jack Haley's Tin Man role in *The Wizard of Oz* if he hadn't been allergic to the metallic makeup. Ebsen later took prime time by storm, first as Davy Crockett's sidekick in the '50s and then as the indelible Jed Clampett, patriarch of *The Beverly Hillbillies,* from 1962 to 1971. Critics saw the family as simpletons; Ebsen disagreed. "They had poise," he said. "They never felt out of place." Nor did the actor. He went on to star again as P.I. Barnaby Jones for seven years. Married three times and the father of seven, Ebsen spent his later years painting rural scenes that he sold online. But show business was his faith. "I never left a dressing room," he once said, "without thanking God for the job."

1926-2003

# Richard Crenna

## HE WAS THE REAL McCOY EARLY—AND TO THE END

Richard Crenna signed up for drama in his L.A. junior high only because "I'd already taken wood shop." The class sparked an unbroken 66-year run that included both TV comic turns in *Our Miss Brooks* and *The Real McCoys* and dramatic film roles such as Sylvester Stallone's boss in the *Rambo* series. At the time of his death from pancreatic cancer, he was back on the tube as Tyne Daly's beau in *Judging Amy.* Crenna, who had three kids with Penni, his wife of 43 years, was, said Garry Marshall, his director on *The Flamingo Kid,* "one of the few gentlemen I met in the business."

1943-2003

# Little Eva

## SHE WAS A NUMBER ONE SOUL SISTER

Eva Boyd, once songwriter Carole King's babysitter, topped the charts as Little Eva with 1962's "The Loco-Motion." She also sang backup for the Drifters and Ben E. King and later worked in a soul-food restaurant in her native North Carolina. "Singing was a wonderful part of my life," she said, "but it wasn't the end of my life."

1947-2003

# Warren Zevon

## BOTH TENDER AND TOUGH, HE CUT A MORDANT MELODY

Diagnosed with terminal cancer while working on his 16th album, *The Wind,* in 2002, Warren Zevon joked, "I've been writing this part for myself for 35 years." Famous for his wild life (he got clean and sober in the '80s) and satirical tunes ("Werewolves of London," "Life'll Kill Ya"), the twice-divorced father of two also composed for TV shows like *Route 66* and *Tales from the Crypt.* Near the end, Zevon, who chose not to undergo treatment, was allowed to eat whatever he wanted. He gorged on ice cream and cookies and got off a typical Zevon zinger: "No more Atkins bars!"

1963-2003

# David Bloom

## A RISING NETWORK NEWS STAR DIED AT 39 WHILE CROSSING THE DESERT IN IRAQ

David Bloom, a *Today* regular since 2000, had a wind-in-the-hair gusto that translated to an immense on-air likability. Whether reporting from the O.J. Simpson trial, Bosnia or the White House, the Minnesota native was so dedicated, said NBC colleague Tim Russert, "you couldn't keep him away from a story." That included an embedded assignment in Iraq, where he died suddenly of a pulmonary embolism. (He had spent days broadcasting from a cramped armored vehicle speeding across the desert.) In a prophetic e-mail, the devout Catholic wrote to his wife, Melanie, mother of their three children, saying he was "saddened by the glimpses of death and destruction . . . but at peace with my God, and with you."

# Robert Atkins

## HE PREACHED THE VALUE OF PROTEIN IN REDUCING THE FAT OF THE LAND

"I want to eradicate obesity and diabetes," Dr. Robert Atkins said shortly before his death (following a fall on an icy sidewalk). "I believe God wants me to do that." Starting with a 1972 megaseller, *Dr. Atkins' Diet Revolution,* the Manhattan cardiologist hooked devotees from Julia Roberts to Sarah Jessica Parker and nabbed a fair chunk of the $35 billion annual weight-loss business by touting steak over spaghetti. Atkins developed the regimen when he cut carbs and dropped 27 lbs. in six weeks as an overweight hospital resident in 1963. But the American Medical Association protested that his high-fat approach could lead to heart disease and kidney problems. Atkins kept fighting, said Veronica, his wife of 15 years, "no matter how much abuse they heaped on him." Finally, a 2002 study very cautiously suggested that Dr. Atkins might be onto something. His regime may still have many dietitians scratching their heads, but for now, you can probably enjoy that bacon cheeseburger—just hold the bun.

# Robert Palmer

## HIS ICONIC MUSIC VIDEOS WERE 'SIMPLY IRRESISTIBLE'

If there were a music video hall of fame, Robert Palmer would be an early inductee. The English rocker's legacy included his "Addicted to Love" and "Simply Irresistible" videos, shot in the mid-'80s with a platoon of poker-faced models. Palmer, who died of a heart attack, molded his dapper image on idols Nat King Cole and Otis Redding and shunned rock excess. "I couldn't see the point of getting up in front of a lot of people when you weren't in control of your wits," he once said. A divorced dad of two, Palmer lived in Switzerland with girlfriend Mary Ambrose. "He was a fabulous singer," said pal Sting. "And underrated."

1949-2003

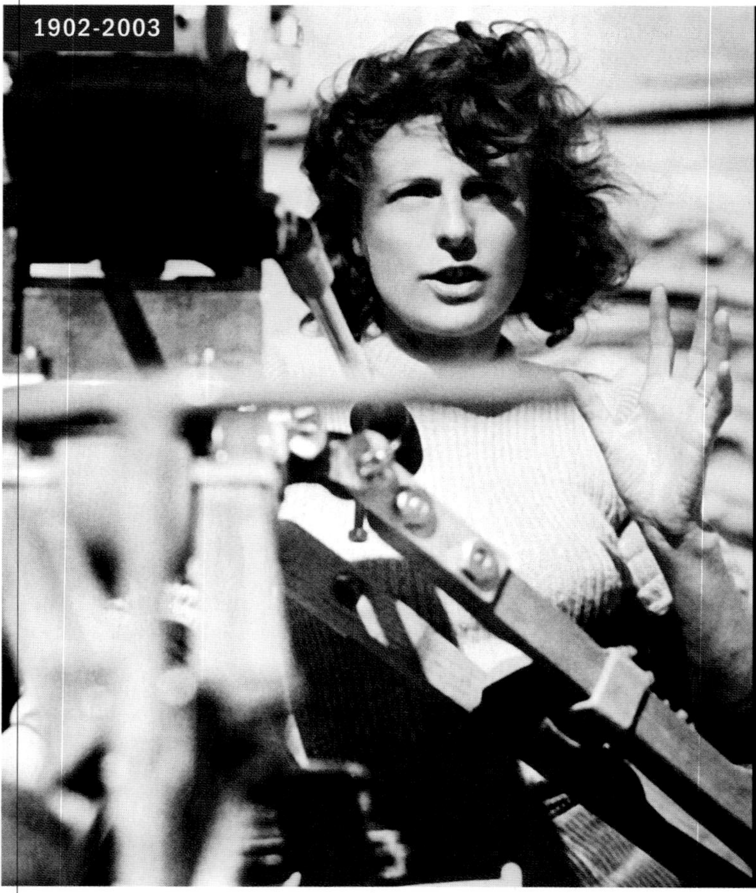

1902-2003

# Leni Riefenstahl

## A GREAT FILMMAKER TARNISHED HER GENIUS GLORIFYING NAZISM

Leni Riefenstahl's *Olympia,* about the 1936 Berlin Summer Games, could have been a model of the documentary art except for one terrible fact. The former dancer, who also filmed *Triumph of the Will,* a stunning—and chilling—look at a 1934 Nazi rally, was Hitler's personal friend and favorite director. She changed her view of Hitler, she said, when she learned of the horrors of his regime during the Allied occupation. Put under house arrest for seven years, she became an artistic untouchable. She later took up still photography, learned to scuba dive at 71 and had a much younger partner, Horst Kettner, now 59. Given her controversial life, she once told a fellow documentary maker, "Death will be a blessed relief."

1920-2003

# David Brinkley

## WITH CANDOR AND IRONY, HE BLAZED THE TRAIL OF TV NEWS

Speaking in his oft-parodied clipped cadences, the succinct—and frequently acerbic—David Brinkley once summed up his five decades in TV news: "11 Presidents, 4 wars, 22 political conventions, 1 moon landing, 2,000 weeks of news, and other stuff on television." "TV grew up, and I happened to be standing there," said Brinkley, originally a newspaper reporter in his native North Carolina. As NBC coanchor with Chet Huntley and later at ABC, where he developed the much-imitated Sunday-morning roundtable *This Week with David Brinkley,* he collected eight Emmys and the Presidential Medal of Freedom. Brinkley, who is survived by second wife Susan and four children, was unequaled covering political conventions. "He created a whole generation of political junkies," said CNN's Jeff Greenfield. "The only way to do news on television is not to be terrified of it," said Brinkley. "Most of the news isn't very important. In fact, very little of it is." A fond good night, David.

1944–2003

# Barry White

## HIS BEDROOM BARITONE PUT ROMANCE TO MUSIC

Serving time in an L.A. jail for stealing tires, teenage gang member Barry White heard Elvis croon "It's Now or Never" on the radio. He took the message to heart and cleaned up his act—and what an act it proved to be. With his velvety R&B voice massaging sultry anthems of seduction like "Can't Get Enough of Your Love, Babe," White sold more than 100 million records. He called his style "lipstick and perfume for the soul." "He drove women absolutely nuts," said pop critic Joel Selvin. "He created an archetype: warm, safe, not threatening. [He was] the Walrus of Love." In the post-disco era his star waned, but by the '90s the twice-wed father of eight had become an icon. His silky tones were part of the soundtrack on *Ally McBeal* and *The Simpsons* and in ads for Apple and AT&T. His aptly named 2000 album *Staying Power* garnered him his first two Grammys. "I'm a doctor no different than one in the biggest hospital," White once said of his appeal. "Except I don't have to cut you to make you feel good."

# Donald O'Connor

1925-2003

## HIS TOES TWINKLED, AND HIS MANTRA WAS 'MAKE 'EM LAUGH'

Fred Astaire was graceful, Gene Kelly was athletic, and Donald O'Connor was a one-man circus. His gravity-defying "Make 'Em Laugh" solo in 1952's *Singin' in the Rain* remains one of the movies' great dance sequences. A son of vaudevillians, he hit the screen at 11 and found fame in the '40s on the back of a talking mule. O'Connor was star of six of the wildly popular *Francis* flicks (the sire of TV's *Mr. Ed*). Then in the '50s he became an Emmy-winning regular on *The Colgate Comedy Hour.* A father of four, O'Connor was wed to second wife Gloria for 47 years. "To be on the same marquee with him," said Broadway's Chita Rivera, who costarred in *Bring Back Birdie,* "means I was keeping extremely good company."

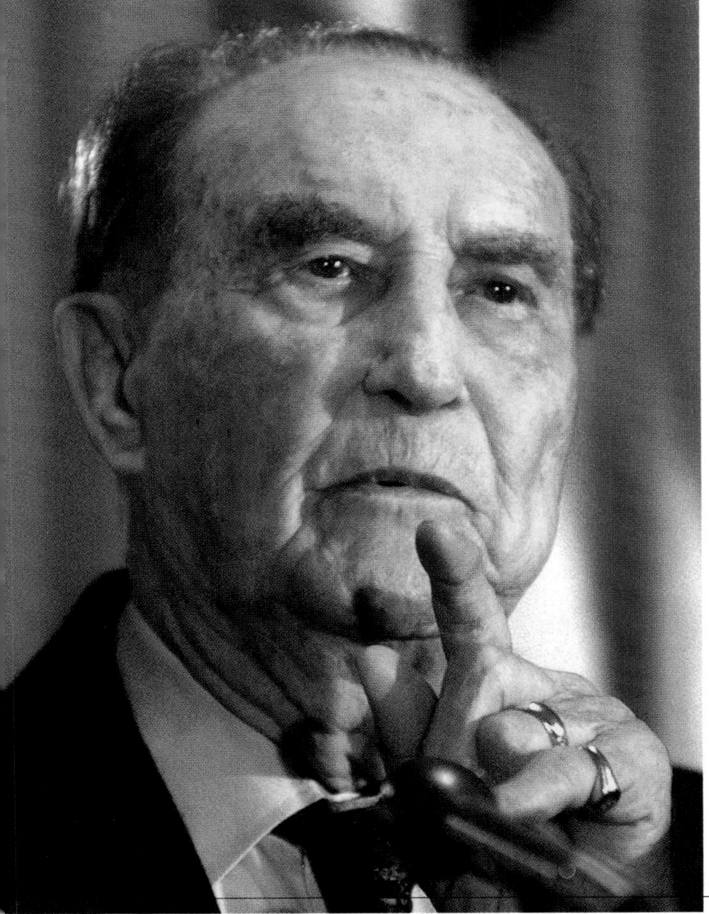

1902-2003

# Strom Thurmond

## A SEGREGATIONIST TURNED REALIST, HE WAS A MAVERICK WHO LIVED ON THE HILL

Still in office at 100, South Carolina's unsinkable Strom Thurmond became the longest-serving U.S. senator in history. He also set the record for lengthiest filibuster—a marathon 24 hours, 18 minutes, to block the civil rights bill of 1957. A decorated WWII vet and self-taught lawyer, he eventually softened his virulent opposition to integration to accommodate political realities. In 1971 he was the first southern senator to hire a black staffer. But his past was a land mine. After toasting Thurmond's '48 run for President (on a racist platform), Senator Trent Lott was forced to resign his leadership post. Thurmond was a fitness buff with an eye for the ladies. He had four children with second wife Nancy, who was 44 years his junior. Asked in '01 to write his own epitaph, the old pol offered, "He loved the people, and the people loved him."

1951-2003

# Fred Berry

## THE 'HEY RAJ' KID GREW UP TO BE A MINISTER BUT NEVER SHED HIS SITCOM PERSONA

With his "Hey Raj" greeting, crowd-pleasing manner and signature red beret and suspenders, a pioneering break-dancer became the breakout star of *What's Happening!!* The '70s sitcom about three teen buddies growing up in L.A. featured Berry as a portly goofball named Rerun—so dubbed because of all the classes he flunked and had to repeat. Berry was so taken by the character (whom he reprised in an updated 1985 series, *What's Happening Now!!*) that he legally changed his name to Fred Rerun Berry. "Rerun" might also describe his domestic life: The father of three split from four wives. He eventually found happiness with Ruby Dianne Blackwell, an actress he had dated back in 1978 and helped cast as his bride in *What's Happening!!* By the time they met again in 2001, Berry had successfully battled drug and alcohol addiction, dropped 108 lbs. and become a Baptist minister. He did don the beret and suspenders again for a cameo in David Spade's '03 comedy *Dickie Roberts: Former Child Star.* Berry, who had diabetes, suffered a stroke before he died at 52. Blackwell, engaged by then to become his fifth wife, decided to place one of his red berets in his casket. "I think Freddie would like that," she said.

1918-2003

# Art Carney

## HE WAS TV'S SIDEKICK OF THE CENTURY

He graced dozens of TV shows and movies, but no role mattered more to Carney—or fans of *The Honeymooners*—than that of Ed Norton, the gangly, guffawing sewer worker and good-natured second banana to blustery Brooklyn bus driver Ralph Kramden (Jackie Gleason). It wasn't just Gleason's admiration of Carney ("The first time I saw the guy act, I knew I'd have to work twice as hard for my laughs," said the Great One) or even the three Emmys Carney won in the classic '50s sitcom. The Mount Vernon, New York-born actor simply loved the character. "Ed was friendly and outgoing, and nothing seemed to bother him," he said. In contrast, Carney fought alcohol and drug problems, which led to a nervous breakdown in 1965 and the end of his 26-year marriage to high school sweetheart Jean Myers, with whom he had three children. By the '70s, Carney had conquered his dependencies, bounced back in a *Honeymooners* revival and copped a Best Actor Oscar for 1974's *Harry and Tonto.* He also (after a shorter second marriage) exchanged vows again with Myers and spent his last 26 years with her.

1931–2003

# Bill Shoemaker

## HE RODE TALL THROUGH A DIFFICULT HOME STRETCH

Over four decades, the 4′11″ jockey everyone called "The Shoe" rode to 8,833 victories, including four Kentucky Derbys, making him the second-winningest rider in history. "Horses just ran for him," said his pal Laffit Pincay Jr. (the all-time champ, with 9,530 wins). In 1991, a year after he retired, a car accident left the thrice-divorced Shoemaker paralyzed from the neck down. He got around in a mouth-controlled wheelchair and worked as a trainer until 1997 (winning 90 races and nearly $3.7 million) to raise his daughter Amanda. He remained upbeat until his death at 72. "You never give up," said Pincay. "There's always another race."

1932–2003

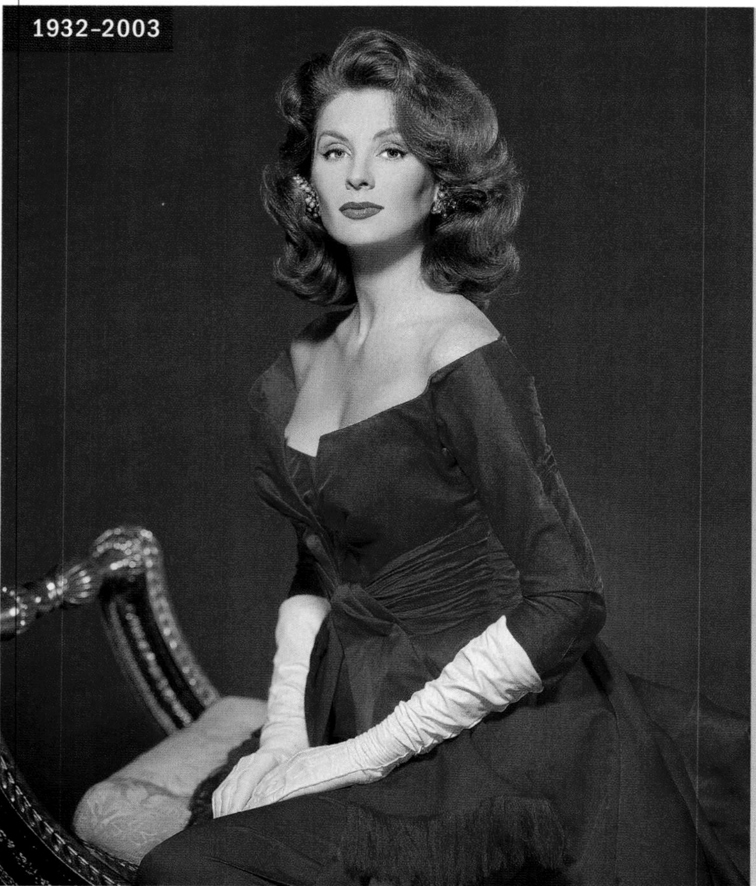

# Suzy Parker

## THE MODEL-ACTRESS GAVE UP CELEBRITY TO RAISE A FAMILY

Long before Heidi Klum, Cheryl Tiegs and even Twiggy, there was Parker, arguably the world's first supermodel and, in the '50s, the highest paid, earning $100,000 a year. After becoming the embodiment of Chanel and posing for numerous magazine covers, Parker leapt to Hollywood, declaring she wanted to be more than just "an animated clothes hanger." Her '57 film debut, *Funny Face,* was followed by *Kiss Them for Me,* opposite Cary Grant, and *Ten North Frederick,* with Gary Cooper. Offscreen her favorite leading man turned out to be actor Bradford Dillman, who became her third husband in 1963. A few years later, she retired from acting to raise the couple's six children (three from their previous marriages). Upon hearing of her death at 70, the eminent photographer Richard Avedon proclaimed, "She invented the form, and no one has surpassed her."

1940–2003

# Bobby Hatfield

## FANS NEVER LOST THEIR LOVIN' FEELIN' FOR BOBBY AND HIS RIGHTEOUS BROTHER BILL

When they first teamed in 1962, Hatfield (left) and partner Bill Medley called themselves the Paramours—until the night a black Marine in the audience saluted their intense R&B stylings by yelling out, "That's righteous, brothers!" "And there it was," said Hatfield, who, dubbed "The Blond Bomber," went on with his fellow Californian to perfect what LIFE magazine called "blue-eyed soul" and to amass 10 Top 40 singles. "You've Lost That Lovin' Feelin'" and "(You're My) Soul and Inspiration" hit No. 1. Though the duo split in 1968, they reteamed in the '80s for concert gigs. Inducted into the Rock and Roll Hall of Fame in March, they were about to launch a new tour in Kalamazoo, Michigan, in November when Hatfield died in his sleep.

1903-2003

# Bob Hope

## TROUPING NONSTOP FROM HOLLYWOOD SETS WITH BING CROSBY TO FAR-FLUNG COMBAT ZONES, A RAT-A-TAT JOKESTER BECAME COMEDY'S KING OF ALL ROADS

England was the birthplace of the famously ski-nosed, sharp-tongued Bob Hope. America was his laugh track. "They once timed me at 44 jokes in four minutes," he boasted—which added up to a lot of jokes in a career that counted 1,145 radio broadcasts, nearly 70 movies, some 500 TV specials, 18 Oscar-hosting gigs plus performances before millions of U.S. troops from World War II to the Gulf War. Leslie Townes Hope (he became Bob because "it's more 'Hiya, fellas,' " he would say) resettled in Cleveland and perfected his timing touring in vaudeville and shooting the *Road* series with Bing Crosby, the granddaddy of the buddy movie. Years before late-night TV, he developed the talk show host prototype: smart and smart-alecky. "His monologues had an enormous influence on me," said Jay Leno. But Hope never found a more adoring audience than the GIs he entertained, sometimes under enemy fire. "He once said that as long as there are troops in a combat area, he could not in good conscience not go," said his USO show writer-director Mort Lachman. Hope (pictured here near Saigon in 1970) made a Christmas tour to Saudi Arabia on the eve of Operation Desert Storm at age 87. At his death of pneumonia, he left behind his wife of 69 years, onetime cabaret singer Dolores, four children and countless fans. Said *Frasier* star Kelsey Grammer: "He gave us 100 years and still left us wanting more." Thanks for the memories.

U.S.ARMY

# Index

"I have so much energy . . . I need to be working all the time," said Britney Spears (in New York City's Times Square). "It feels normal to me."

"Servicemen audiences were so responsive that it was hard for me to give up," recalled Bob Hope (here in 1944) of his World War II tours.

# Photo Credits

## Table of Contents

**3** (clockwise from top left) Rafael-Pixel Presse/London Features; Robert Trachtenberg/ABC; Larsen & Talbert; Carlo Allegri/Getty; Kevin Mazur/Wireimage

## People of the Year

**5** Dan MacMedan/Wireimage **6-7** Stephen Savoia/AP **8-9** Rex USA **10-11** Rex USA **12** Courtesy Peterson Family **13** (from left) Martin Adams/ Zuma; Gamma; Jerome T. Nakagawa/ AP **14-15** Dennis Van Tine/London Features **16** (from top) Guillermo Arias/AP; Dan Habib/Corbis Saba **17** Roger L. Wollenberg/UPI/Landov **18** (clockwise from top left) Mickey Welsh/AP; Dave Martin/AP; Kathy Willens/AP **19** Erik C. Pendzich/Rex USA **20** (from top) Rick Bowmer/AP; Gregg Deguire/Wireimage **21** (from left) Ida Mae Astute/ABC/AP; Michael Winston/Wireimage **22** Kevin Mazur/ Wireimage **23** (from top) Rex USA; Vaughn Youtz/Zuma **24** AFP/ Corbis **25** Spencer Platt/Getty **26** F. Scott Schafer/Corbis Outline **27** (clockwise from left) John Stillwell/ EPA; London Bureau (4) **28** Stefano C. Montesi/Photomovie/Retna **29** Nick Cornish/Rex USA **30** Jive Records **31** Lee Celano/Wireimage **32** Jeff Klein/ Zuma **33** Russell Boyce/Reuters/ Corbis **34-35** Matthias Clamer **36** (from top) Miranda Shen/Celebrity Photo; Courtesy James White **37** Kevin Knight/Corbis Outline **38** Andrew Mac-pherson/Corbis Outline **39** Neal Preston **40** Larsen & Talbert **41** Gregg Deguire/Wireimage **42** Lance Staedler/Warner Bros. **43** Tim Rooke/ Rex USA **44** Flynet Pictures **45** Courtesy Nigel Parry/Warner Bros. **46** (from top) Chris O'Meara/AP; David Wilson Burnham/Getty **47** (from left) Kevin Winter/Getty; Gary C. Caskey/ Reuters **48-49** Photo Illustration Albert Watson **50** Corbis Outline **51** (from top) Lyle Stafford/Reuters/ Landov; Elaine Thompson/Zuma **52** Robert Maxwell/CPi/Art Dept. **53** Jonathan Evans/Rex USA **54-55** Gabriel Bouys/AFP/Getty

## Shock and Awe

**57** Rex USA **58-59** Jordan Van Aken/Zuma **60** Blake Sell/Reuters/ Landov **61** NASA/Getty **62** (from top) Kin Cheung/Reuters; Robert E. Klein/AP **63** Sean M. Haffrey/ San Diego Union Tribune/Zuma

## Milestones

**64** (from left) Getty; Sipa; Win McNamee/Reuters/Landov **65** Coconut Coast Weddings **66** (from top) Carmen Valdes/Retna; Virginia Sherwood/ABC **67** Jim Lee/AAP **68** (from top) Courtesy Tyler & Langdon; Courtesy Denis Reggie **69** (from top) Jean Patrick/Sipa; Harold Hechler/ Retna **70** (from top) Brian Marcus/ Fred Marcus Inc.; Mikel Healey **71** (clockwise from left) Crawford Brown/Mirrorpix; Serge Thomann; Serge Thomann/Wireimage **72** Getty **73** (from top) Santiago; Joe Buissink/ Wireimage **74-75** (clockwise from bottom left) Dimitrios Kambouris/Wire-image; Mishan Andre/AP; Kevin Mazur/ Wireimage; Joe Buissink/Wireimage **76** Mike McCartney/Camera Press/ Retna **77** Ramey **78-79** (clockwise from top left) Kevin Mazur/Wireimage; Capital Pictures/Retna; Larry Busacca/ Wireimage; Willi Schneider/Rex USA; Sipa; Patrick Giardino/Corbis **80** (from top) Dave Parker/Alpha/Globe; Daniele Venturelli/Reflex News **81** (from left) Ronette Riley; CBS/AP **82** Mike Lawn/Rex USA **83** (from top) Lawrence Schwartzwald/Splash News; Joseph Marzullo/Retna **84-85** (clock-wise from bottom left) Scott Weiner/ Retna; John B. Zissel/Ipol; Jeff Kravitz/ Film Magic; Stuart Ramson/AP; Joy E. Scheller/London Features **86** Janet Gough/Celebrity Photo **87** (from top) Janet Gough/Celebrity Photo; Kevin Reece/Wireimage **88-89** (clockwise from bottom left) Gilbert Flores/Celeb-rity Photo (2); Steve Granitz/Wireimage; Adam Nemser/Photolink; Nesti Mendoza

## Hollywood's Big Nights

**91** (clockwise from top) John Lazar/Wireimage; Michael Caulfield/ Wireimage; Wenn; Ray Mickshaw/ Wireimage **92-93** (from left) Kevin Winter/Getty; Vinnie Zuffante/Starfile; Steve Granitz/Wireimage; Kim Johnson/AP; Fitzroy Barrett/Globe **94-95** (from left) Jeff Christensen/ Reuters/Landov; Scott Gries/Getty; Jeff Christensen/Reuters; Globe **96-97** (from left) Frank Trapper/Corbis; Tsuni/Gamma; Mike Blake/Reuters; Steve Granitz/Wireimage; David Edwards/Daily Celeb **98-99** (from left) Kevin Mazur/Wireimage; Fitzroy Barrett/Globe; James Smeal/Galella; Gaboury/DMI/Rex USA; Frank Micelotta/ Getty; Axelle/Bauer-Griffin **100-101** (from left) Steve Granitz/Wireimage; Fitzroy Barrett/Globe; Calvin Moore/ Kika Press; Jon Kopaloff/Getty; Gilbert Flores/Celebrity Photo; Janet Gough/ Celebrity Photo **102-103** (from left) Janet Gough/Celebrity Photo; Jen Lowery/London Features (2); Fitzroy Barrett/Globe; Gregg Deguire/Wire-image; Gilbert Flores/Celebrity Photo

## Tributes

**104** Neal Peters Collection **106-107** Corbis Outline **108-109** Photofest **110-111** Andrew Southam/CPi **112** Reg Innell/Toronto Star/Zuma **113** JDEV/JPI **114** Reynolds T/Corbis Sygma **116-117** (clockwise from bottom left) Time Life/Getty; Everett; Getty; Henry Grossman/Time Life/ Getty **118** Globe **119** (from top) Getty; Glenn Campbell/Shooting Star **120** (from left) Kobal; Ernest Reshovsky/ MPTV **121** (from top) Michael Ochs Archive; Barry King/Ipol **122** NBC/ Globe **123** (from top) Hulton/Getty; Jim Wells/AP **124** (from top) Henry Leutwyler/Corbis; Heinz Kluetmeier/SI **125** Photofest **126** (from top) Screen-scenes; Mario Casilli/MPTV **127** Karsh/Globe **128** Photofest **129** (from top) SMP/Globe; Redferns/ Retna **130** (from top) Neal Preston/ Corbis; Courtesy Erin Fogarty **131** Pieter Van Hattem/CPi **132** (from top) TJ Collection/Shooting Star; AFP/ Getty **133** NBC/Globe **134** David Redfern/Retna **135** (from top) John Swope/Time Life/Getty; Terry Ashe/ Time Life/Getty **136** MPTV **137** Jack Stager/Globe **138** (from top) Aaron Rapoport/Corbis; Kobal **139** Globe **140-141** AP

## Index

**142** Kevin Mazur/Wireimage **143** Kobal

## Cover

Sonia Moskowitz/Globe; **Insets, from top:** Roger Karnbad/Celebrity Photo; Steve Granitz/Wireimage; Chris Polk/Film Magic; Pascal Le Segretain/Getty; Carlo Allegri/Getty; Brian Zak/Polaris; **Back Cover:** Stephan Savoia/AP